Rome

COLLINS
Glasgow & London

3009
IVECO

First published 1990

Published by William Collins Sons & Company Limited
Printed in Hong Kong
ISBN 0 00 435785-X

HOW TO USE THIS BOOK

Your Collins Traveller Guide will help you find your way around your chosen destination quickly and easily. It is colour-coded for easy reference:

The blue-coded 'topic' section answers the question 'I would like to see or do something; where do I go and what do I see when I get there?' A simple, clear layout provides an alphabetical list of activities and events, offers you a selection of each, tells you how to get there, what it will cost, when it is open and what to expect. Each topic in the list has its own simplified map, showing the position of each item and the nearest landmark or transport access, for instant orientation. Whether your interest is Churches or Restaurants you can find all the information you need quickly and simply. Where major resorts within an area require in-depth treatment, they follow the main topics section in alphabetical order.

The red-coded section is a lively and informative gazetteer. In one alphabetical list you can find essential facts about the main places and cultural items - 'What is La Bastille?', 'Who was Michelangelo?' - as well as practical and invaluable travel information. It covers everything you need to know to help you enjoy yourself and get the most out of your time away, from Accommodation through Babysitters, Car Hire, Food, Health, Money, Newspapers, Taxis and Telephones to Zoos.

Cross-references: Type in small capitals - **CHURCHES** - tells you that more information on an item is available within the topic on churches. A-Z in bold - **A-Z** - tells you that more information is available on an item within the gazetteer. Simply look under the appropriate heading. A name in bold - **Holy Cathedral** - also tells you that more information on an item is available in the gazetteer under that particular heading.

Packed full of information and easy to use - you'll always know where you are with your Collins Traveller Guide!

Photographs by **Michael Dent & Keith Allardyce**

INTRODUCTION

Rome, the Eternal City, is an extraordinary collaboration between the ancient and modern, the sacred and profane, and the sublime and preposterous, guaranteed to induce in the visitor an array of emotions ranging from rapture to despair. Ancient ruins of temples and buildings which once echoed to the footsteps of Julius Caesar and Augustus, are assaulted by the noise and pollution of the city traffic only metres away; pilgrims from every nation crowd St Peter's square in homage to the seat of Christendom, whilst news kiosks on every street corner display acres of pornographic magazines and comics; the city's churches, palaces and museums house masterpieces by Raphael, Michelangelo and Bernini, yet in the outskirts lies EUR, Mussolini's abortive attempt to eclipse the achievements of Classical and Renaissance Rome, filled with bleak authoritarian concrete structures devoid of aesthetic quality or interest, save as stark symbols of Fascism's corruption of human creativity. These contrasts affirm that the city, perhaps more than any other, is a living witness to the triumphs and tragedies of human history: and to visit Rome, which has miraculously survived throughout the litany of invasions, wars, political and religious upheavals, and the contemporary evils of bureaucracy, corruption and exhaust fumes, is one of life's great experiences.

The rise of Rome from its humble origins to become the *caput mundi*, 'capital of the world', whose laws, technology, culture and religion spread throughout the known globe is a story of enduring fascination. Archeological evidence suggests that the city began as a small farming community on the Palatine at least a century before its supposed mythical foundation by Romulus in 753 BC. The collaboration of this pastoral community with rival tribes sparked the growth of the city under the Sabine and then Etruscan kings. After the founding of the Republic in 509, a series of defensive wars against attacking tribes evolved into aggressive campaigns of expansion, including the defeat of Carthage (146 BC) and Caesar's expeditions against Gaul and Britain (58-53 BC), until under Trajan the empire reached its greatest extent, bestraddling the known world from the Atlantic to the Black Sea. Recurrent political instability and economic decay combined with external attacks by barbarian tribes gradually weakened the Empire, divided into East and West by Diocletian in 286, until in 476 the last emperor, Romulus

Augustulus, was deposed by the German Odoacer. During the Dark Ages, as European princes, aristocratic Italian families and the Papacy struggled for possession of the city, the population of Rome dwindled from one million at the height of the Empire to less than 20,000 in the 12thC. In 1308 Pope Clement V transferred the papal residence to Avignon, and through the ensuing decades of the French exile and then the Great Schism, the city fell into a pitiable state, its crumbling monuments surrounded by filth and squalour. It was not until the return of Pope Martin V in 1420 that the city began to revive and interest in the classical age began to resurface, until under the pontificates of Julius II and Leo X the city emerged at the centre of Renaissance art and culture. The brutal Sack of Rome by German and Spanish troops in 1527 blunted Renaissance optimism, but the city survived and, fuelled by the Counter Reformation in the 16th and 17thCs, witnessed the splendours of the Baroque embodied in the construction of new churches, palaces, fountains and streets under the presiding genius of Bernini. In the 19thC the Risorgimento led by Garibaldi and Mazzini eventually united Italy under the House of Savoy, confining the political power of the Papacy to the Vatican, and in 1870 Rome was declared the capital of the new nation. In the 20thC the city has survived Mussolini's dictatorship and mercifully escaped serious bombardment in the Second World War. Rome's attractions are such that within the limits of a brief stay, to identify each important ruin or visit every notable church and palace, to explore all the museums or wander through every attractive square or medieval street, would be impossible. There are however certain priorities: at the heart of the ancient city are the Palatine and Forum, filled with ruined temples, palaces and civic buildings in which figures such as Caesar and Anthony, Augustus and Livia and their imperial successors once worshipped, entertained and governed; unforgettable too is the Colosseum, scene of spectacular and savage entertainments, and the Pantheon, masterpiece of Roman architecture. Despite reconstruction, churches such as Santa Maria Maggiore, with its magnificent gilded coffered ceiling or Santa Prassede, containing exquisite 9thC mosaics, retain the imprint of their early Christian origins. Evocative of the medieval city is the simple Romanesque church of S Maria in Cosmedin, or the Piazza Campo dei Fiori and the surrounding streets and buildings of the medieval quarter. Dating from the Renaissance is the impressive Palazzo Farnese, Michelangelo's Piazza del Campidoglio and his moving *Pietà* in St Peter's. From the Baroque age, whose monuments saturate the city, are Bernini's delightful fountains, his magnificent contributions to the interior of St Peter's, and outside the basilica, his famous colonnaded Piazza. No visit to the city can be complete without a tour of the Vatican Museums, which house the world's most valuable treasures from every age, including the *Apollo Belvedere*, the *Laocoön*, Raphael's frescoed *stanzi*, and Michelangelo's ceiling and *Last Judgement* in the Sistine Chapel.

Mixed with the pleasures of the above are various less enjoyable aspects of the city's character. The traffic makes walking hazardous - crossing the road can become an unequal gladiatorial combat between flesh and machine; eagerly anticipated tourist attractions are often undergoing restoration, shrouded from view by scaffolding and green netting; cafés charge exorbitant sums for the privilege of sitting down, not ideal for weary sightseers seeking respite from the summer heat; in some restaurants waiters seem to take pride in ignoring or humiliating hapless visitors unfamiliar with the language and ritual of Italian meals; and similar grudging service is sometimes thought sufficient by shop-keepers and public officials.

These minor nuisances, however, should not prove any real deterrent when considering the historic, artistic and cultural treasures Rome has to offer - which is the reason why the city has always been, and will always remain, a place of pilgrimage for countless travellers.

Callum Brines

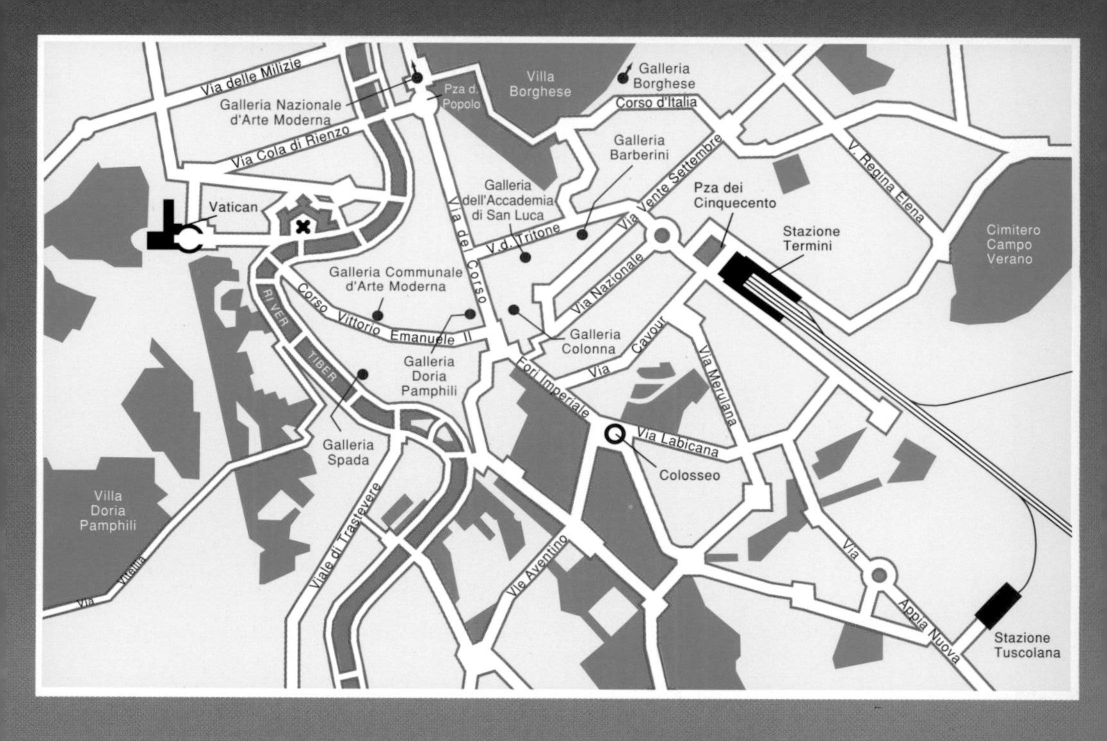

Via delle Milizie
Galleria Nazionale d'Arte Moderna
Pza d. Popolo
Villa Borghese
Galleria Borghese
Corso d'Italia
Via Cola di Rienzo
Galleria Barberini
Via Vente Settembre
V. Regina Elena
Pza dei Cinquecento
Cimitero Campo Verano
Vatican
Galleria dell'Accademia di San Luca
Via del Corso
V.d. Tritone
Stazione Termini
Via Nazionale
Galleria Communale d'Arte Moderna
Corso Vittorio Emanuele II
RIVER TIBER
Galleria Colonna
Via Cavour
Via Merulana
Galleria Doria Pamphili
Fori Imperiale
Via Labicana
Colosseo
Galleria Spada
Villa Doria Pamphili
Viale di Trastevere
Vie Aventino
Via Vitellia
Via Appia Nuova
Stazione Tuscolana

GALLERIA BORGHESE Villa Borghese, Viale dell'Uccelliera.
•0900-1330 Mon.-Sat., 0930-1230 Sun. M Spagna.
Masterpieces by Bernini, Canova, Raphael, Titian and Caravaggio. See **A-Z**.

GALLERIA BARBERINI Palazzo Barberini, Via Quattro Fontane 13.
•0900-1300 Sun.-Fri., 0900-1400 Sat. M Barberini. •L. 3000.
The major national collection. Includes Raphael's La Fornarina. *See* **A-Z**.

GALLERIA DORIA-PAMPHILI Piazza del Collegio Romano 1.
•1000-1300 Tues. & Fri.-Sun. Bus 60, 62, 87, 88. •L. 2000.
The richest private collection in Rome. See **A-Z**.

GALLERIA SPADA Palazzo Spada, Via Capo di Ferro.
•0900-1400 Tues.-Sat., 0900-1300 Sun. Bus 26, 44, 60. •L. 2000.
Small but interesting collection, including works by Titian and Rubens.

GALLERIA COLONNA Palazzo Colonna, Via della Pilotta 17.
•0900-1300 Sat. only. Closed Aug. Bus 60, 62, 85. •L. 3000.
Private collection including Portrait of a Nobleman *by Veronese.*

GALLERIA DELL'ACCADEMIA DI SAN LUCA
Piazza dell'Accademia di San Luca 77.
•1000-1300 Mon., Wed., Fri. M Barberini. •L. 2000.
Works by Raphael and Rubens; spiral staircase by Borromini (see **A-Z**).

GALLERIA NAZIONALE D'ARTE MODERNA
Villa Borghese, Viale delle Belle Arti 131.
•0900-1400 Tues., Wed., Fri.; 0900-1800 Thurs., Sat.; 0900-1300 Sun.
M Flaminio. •L. 3000.
Large collection of Italian art dating from the 19thC to the present. See **A-Z**.

GALLERIA COMMUNALE D'ARTE MODERNA
Palazzo Braschi, Piazza S Pantaleo 10.
•0900-1400 Tues.-Sat. (and 1700-2000 Wed., Thurs.), 0900-1300 Sun.
Bus 46, 52, 64. •L. 3000.
19thC Roman art, including watercolours by Bartolomeo Pinelli.

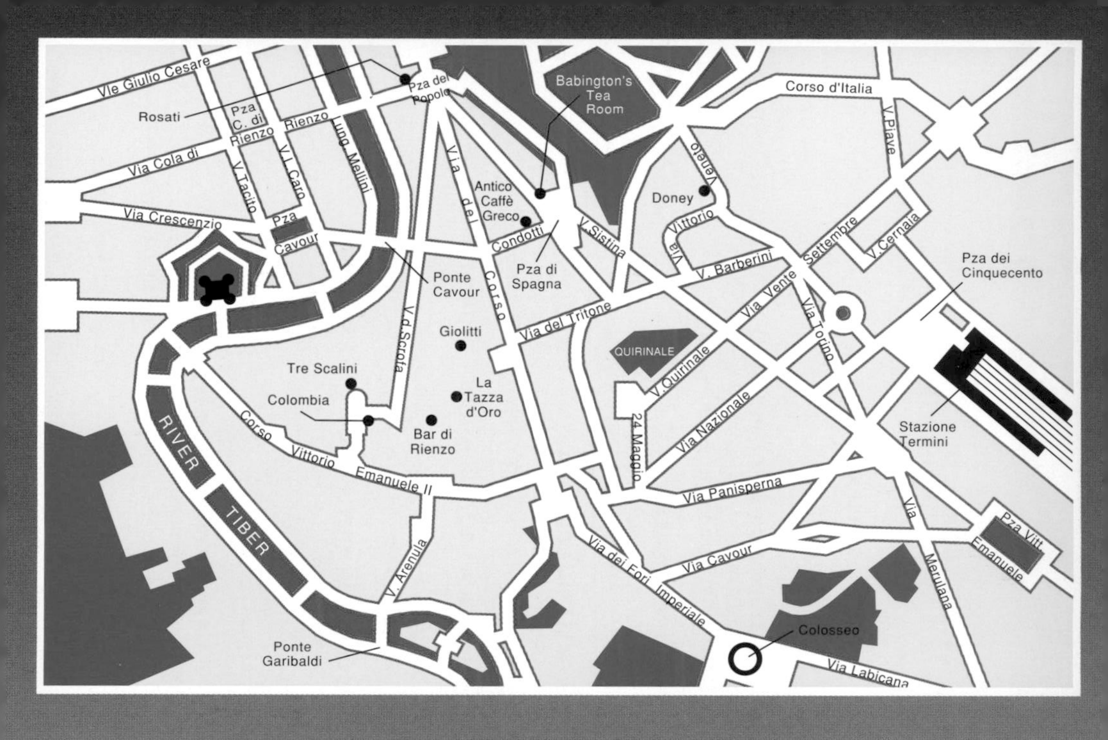

Vle Giulio Cesare
Pza del Popolo
Babington's Tea Room
Corso d'Italia
Rosati
Pza C. di Rienzo
Rienzo
Via Cola di
V.Tacito
V.L.Caro
Lung. Mellini
Via Crescenzio
Pza Cavour
Via del Corso
Antico Caffè Greco
Condotti
Pza di Spagna
V.Sistina
Doney
Veneto
Via Vittorio
V.Piave
Settembre
V.Cernaia
Pza dei Cinquecento
Ponte Cavour
V.d.Scrofa
Giolitti
Via del Tritone
V. Barberini
Via Venti
Via Torino
QUIRINALE
V.Quirinale
Tre Scalini
Colombia
La Tazza d'Oro
Bar di Rienzo
24 Maggio
Via Nazionale
Stazione Termini
Corso Vittorio Emanuele II
Via Panisperna
Via Merulana
Pza Vitt. Emanuele
RIVER TIBER
V. Arenula
Via dei Fori Imperiale
Via Cavour
Colosseo
Ponte Garibaldi
Via Labicana

ANTICO CAFFÈ GRECO Via Condotti 86.
• 0800-2100 Mon.-Sat. M Spagna.
The decor dates from 1860, when this was a favourite haunt of writers, artists and musicians.

DONEY Via Vittorio Veneto 145.
• 0800-1300, 1600-2000 Tues.-Sun. M Barberini/Spagna.
Fashionable pavement café on the famous Via Veneto *(see* CITY DISTRICTS*).*

COLOMBIA Piazza Navona 88.
• 0700-0130 Tues.-Sun. Bus 26, 81.
Admire the Piazza Navona *(see* SQUARES, **A-Z***)* *over a cup of fine coffee.*

ROSATI Piazza del Popolo 4.
• 0800-0100 Wed.-Mon. M Flaminio.
Offers excellent cocktails, and a wide choice of pastries and cakes.

BABINGTON'S TEA ROOM Piazza di Spagna 23.
• 0900-2030 Fri.-Wed. M Spagna.
Quite expensive, but popular for English-style tea, scones and muffins.

TRE SCALINI Piazza Navona 30.
• 0700-0230 Thurs.-Tues. Bus 26, 81.
Serves the best tartufo *in town (chocolate ice-cream with a hint of truffle).*

GIOLITTI Via Uffici del Vicario 40.
• 0700-0200 Tues.-Sun. Bus 26, 81.
Recognized for 30 years as the king of Rome's ice-cream makers.

BAR DI RIENZO Piazza della Rotonda 9.
• 0730-0230 Wed.-Mon. Bus 26, 81.
Offers the choice of a full English breakfast or the traditional cappuccino.

LA TAZZA D'ORO Via degli Orfani 86.
• 0700-2200 Mon.-Sat. Bus 26, 81.
Try some of the best coffee in Rome - ristretto *(strong), or* freddo *(iced).*

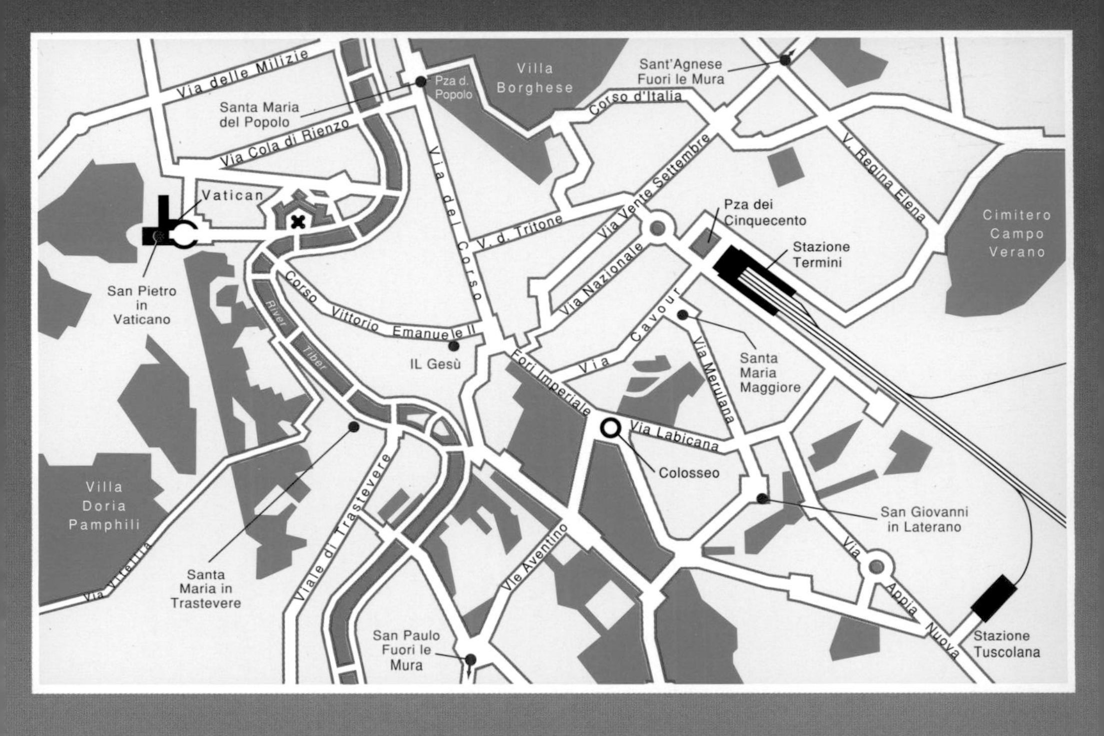

Via delle Milizie
Pza d. Popolo
Villa Borghese
Sant'Agnese Fuori le Mura
Santa Maria del Popolo
Corso d'Italia
Via Cola di Rienzo
V. Regina Elena
Via del Corso
Vatican
Via Vente Settembre
Pza dei Cinquecento
Cimitero Campo Verano
V. d. Tritone
Stazione Termini
San Pietro in Vaticano
Via Nazionale
Corso Vittorio Emanuele II
Via Cavour
River Tiber
Santa Maria Maggiore
IL Gesù
Via Merulana
Fori Imperiale
Via Labicana
Colosseo
Villa Doria Pamphili
San Giovanni in Laterano
Viale di Trastevere
Vle Aventino
Via Appia Nuova
Via Vitellia
Santa Maria in Trastevere
San Paulo Fuori le Mura
Stazione Tuscolana

SAN PIETRO IN VATICANO (ST PETER'S)
Piazza S Pietro, Città del Vaticano.
•0700-1900 (summer), 0700-1800 (winter) daily.
Crypt (Grottoes) closed 1300-1430. M Ottaviano, Bus 64.
Famous symbol of Christendom, built over the tomb of St Peter. See **A-Z**.

SAN GIOVANNI IN LATERANO Piazza S Giovanni in Laterano.
•0700-1830 daily. M San Giovanni.
The Cathedral Church of Rome, with a beautiful interior designed by Borromini (see **A-Z**). *See* **A-Z**.

SANTA MARIA MAGGIORE Piazza S Maria Maggiore.
•0700-1900 daily. M Termini.
One of the great patriarchal churches. The gilt ceiling is reputedly made from gold brought back by the first explorers of America. See WALK 2, **A-Z**.

SAN PAOLO FUORI LE MURA Via di S Paolo/Via Ostiense 190.
•0700-1900 daily. M San Paolo.
The second great basilica after St Peter's (see **San Pietro in Vaticano**).

IL GESÙ Piazza del Gesù, off Corso Vittorio Emanuele II.
•0600-1230, 1600-1915 daily. Bus 56, 60, 62, 64.
Rome's principal Jesuit church - St Ignatius Loyola is buried here. See **Gesù**.

SANTA MARIA IN TRASTEVERE Piazza S Maria in Trastevere.
•0800-1900 daily. Bus 56, 60,170.
The first church in Rome to be dedicated to the Virgin. See WALK 3.

SANTA MARIA DEL POPOLO Piazza del Popolo.
•0700-1230, 1600-1900 daily. M Flaminio.
Contains works by Bernini, Raphael and Caravaggio. See **A-Z**.

SANT'AGNESE FUORI LE MURA Via Nomentana 349.
•1000-1200, 1600-1730 Mon.-Sat. Bus 36, 60, 62.
Endowed by Constantia, daughter of the Emperor Constantine (see **A-Z**), *in the 4thC. Retains many original features.*

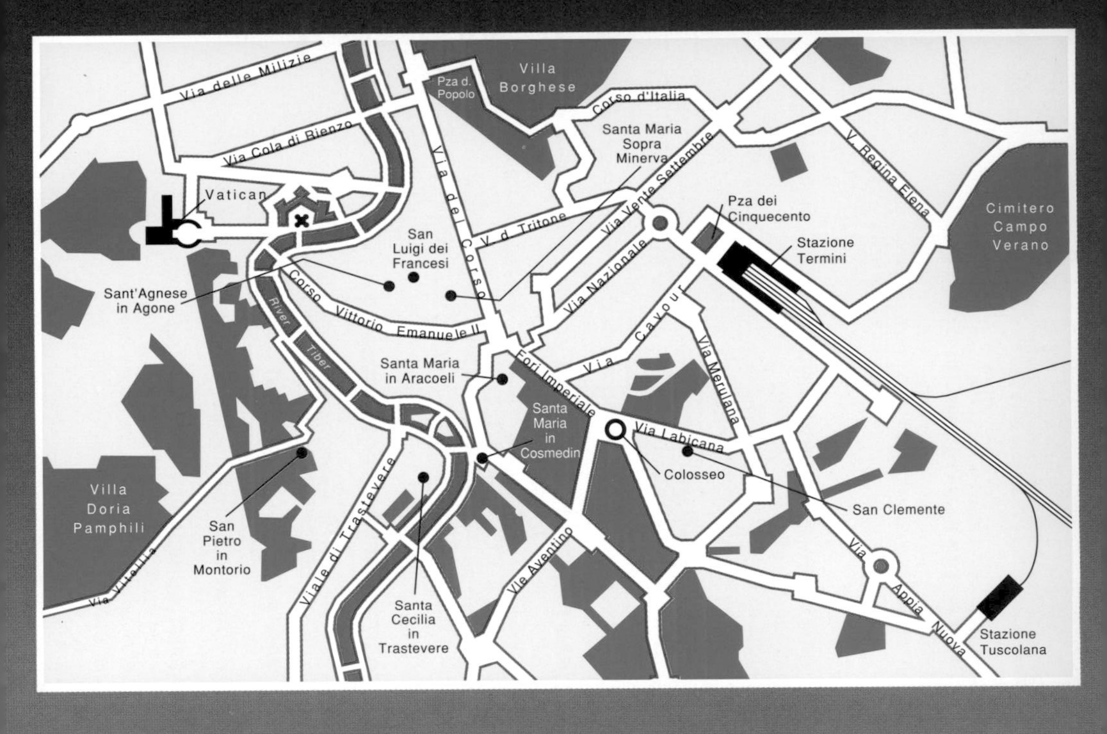
Via delle Milizie
Villa Borghese
Pza d. Popolo
Corso d'Italia
Via Cola di Rienzo
Santa Maria Sopra Minerva
V. Regina Elena
Vatican
Via del Corso
V. d. Tritone
Via Vente Settembre
Pza dei Cinquecento
Cimitero Campo Verano
Stazione Termini
San Luigi dei Francesi
Via Nazionale
Sant'Agnese in Agone
Corso Vittorio Emanuele II
River Tiber
Via Cavour
Via Merulana
Santa Maria in Aracoeli
Fori Imperiale
Santa Maria in Cosmedin
Via Labicana
Colosseo
San Clemente
Villa Doria Pamphili
San Pietro in Montorio
Via Vitellia
Viale di Trastevere
Vle Aventino
Via Appia Nuova
Santa Cecilia in Trastevere
Stazione Tuscolana

SANT'AGNESE IN AGONE Piazza Navona.
•1700-1900 Mon.-Sat., 1000-1300, 1600-1900 Sun. Bus 62, 64, 70.
Built on the site of St Agnes' martyrdom. Facade by Borromini (see **A-Z***).*

SANTA CECILIA IN TRASTEVERE
Piazza di Santa Cecilia, off Via dei Genovesi.
•0700-1200, 1600-1900 daily. Bus 23, 26, 44, 170.
Contains Cavallini's superb The Last Judgement *(1293). See* **WALK 3**.

SAN CLEMENTE Piazza di S Clemente.
•Lower church open 0900-1130, 1530-1800 Mon.-Sat.,1000-1130, 1530-1830 Sun. M Colosseo.
Combination of 4thC and 12thC churches and earlier remains. See **A-Z**.

SAN LUIGI DEI FRANCESI Piazza S Luigi dei Francesi.
•0700-1200, 1600-1900. Bus 26, 70 to Corso del Rinascimento.
Contains Caravaggio's (see **A-Z***) cycle of paintings on the life of St Matthew.*

SANTA MARIA IN ARACOELI Piazza d'Aracoeli.
•0700-1200, 1600-1730 daily. Bus 26, 44, 90, 170.
Inside are magnificent frescoes by Pinturicchio, and an olive-wood image of the Santo Bambino *(Holy Child) said to heal sick children. See* **A-Z**.

SANTA MARIA IN COSMEDIN Piazza Bocca della Verità.
•0700-1200, 1600-1900. Bus 28, 29, 90, 92, 94.
The most beautiful medieval church in Rome. See **WALK 3**, **A-Z**.

SANTA MARIA SOPRA MINERVA Piazza della Minerva.
•0700-1200, 1600-1900 daily. Bus 26, 87, 94.
Rome's only Gothic church. See **WALK 4**.

SAN PIETRO IN MONTORIO
Piazza San Pietro in Montorio, Via Garibaldi.
•0700-1200, 1600-1730 daily. Bus 41, 44.
15thC church with frescoes by Sebastiano del Piombo, and Bramante's (see **A-Z***) famous* Tempietto. *See* **A-Z**.

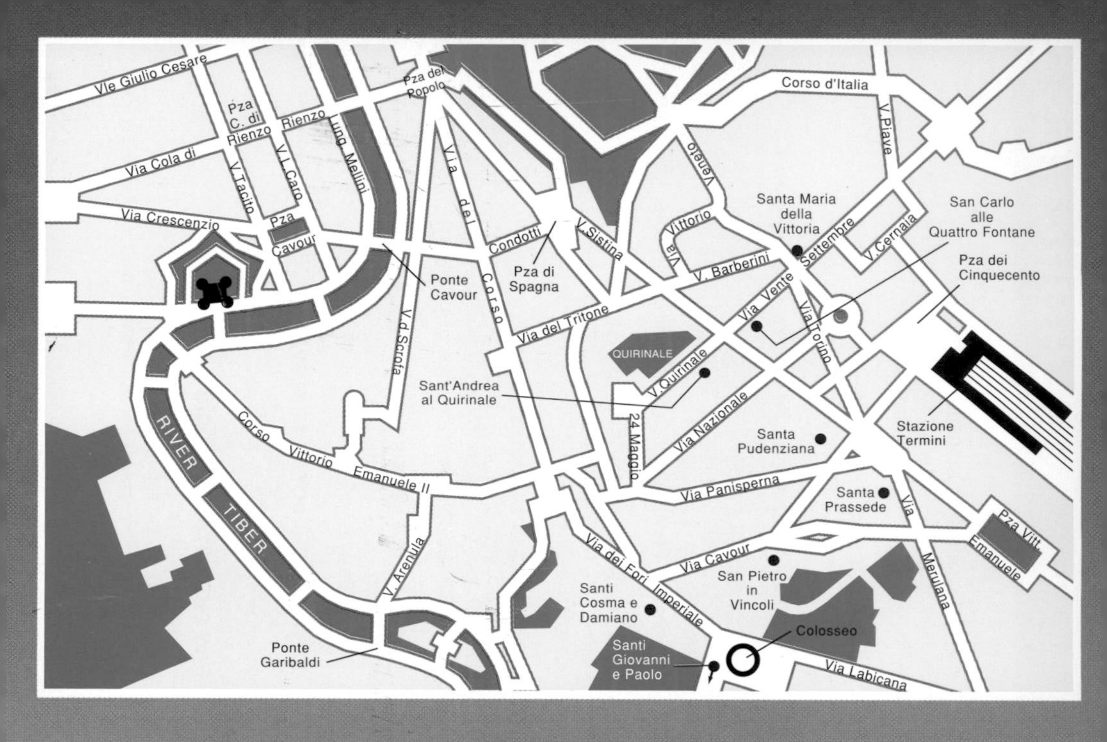
Vle Giulio Cesare
Pza del Popolo
Corso d'Italia
Pza C. di Rienzo
Rienzo
Lung. Mellini
Via Cola di
V.L.Caro
V.Tacito
Via Crescenzio
Pza Cavour
Via del Corso
V.Piave
Veneto
Santa Maria della Vittoria
San Carlo alle Quattro Fontane
Settembre
V. Cernaia
Pza dei Cinquecento
Condotti
Pza di Spagna
V.Sistina
Via Vittorio
V. Barberini
Via Vente
Via Torino
Ponte Cavour
V.d.Scrofa
Via del Tritone
QUIRINALE
V. Quirinale
Sant'Andrea al Quirinale
Via Nazionale
Stazione Termini
Santa Pudenziana
24 Maggio
Corso Vittorio Emanuele II
RIVER TIBER
Via Panisperna
Santa Prassede
Via Merulana
Pza Vitt. Emanuele
Via dei Fori Imperiale
Via Cavour
San Pietro in Vincoli
Santi Cosma e Damiano
V. Arenula
Colosseo
Santi Giovanni e Paolo
Ponte Garibaldi
Via Labicana

SANT'ANDREA AL QUIRINALE Via del Quirinale 29.
• 0800-1200, 1400-1900 Wed.-Mon. M Barberini.
Small oval church designed by Bernini (see **A-Z***) in 1671.*

SAN CARLO ALLE QUATTRO FONTANE Via del Quirinale 23.
• 0900-1230 Mon.-Sat. M Barberini.
This tiny church is probably Borromini's (see **A-Z***) finest work. Interesting to compare it with the nearby Sant'Andrea, by his rival Bernini (see* **A-Z***).*

SANTI COSMA E DAMIANO Via dei Fori Imperiali.
• 0700-1300, 1430-1900 daily. M Colosseo.
6thC church with splendid mosaics. See **WALK 1**.

SANTI GIOVANNI E PAOLO
Clivo di Scauro, off Via di San Gregorio.
• 0700-1200, 1600-1900 daily. M Circo Massimo.
Built on the site of the murder of John and Paul, two imperial officers under Constantine II martyred by his successor Julian the Apostate in the 4thC.

SANTA MARIA DELLA VITTORIA Via XX Settembre.
• 0700-1200, 1600-1930 daily. M Repubblica.
See the Cornaro Chapel by Bernini (see **A-Z***), a Baroque extravaganza.*

SAN PIETRO IN VINCOLI Piazza San Pietro in Vincoli.
• 0700-1300, 1430-1900 daily. M Cavour.
Houses the chains with which St Peter was bound during his captivity in Jerusalem, and Moses *by Michelangelo (see* **A-Z***). See* **WALK 2**, **A-Z**.

SANTA PRASSEDE Via Santa Prassede 9 (off Via Merulana).
• 0730-1200, 1600-1800 daily. M Cavour.
See the Chapel of St Zeno with its beautiful Byzantine mosaics. See **WALK 2**.

SANTA PUDENZIANA Via Urbana 161.
• 0730-1200, 1600-1800 Mon.-Sat. M Cavour.
Contains a splendid mosaic showing Christ surrounded by his Apostles, and the two sisters, Prassede and Pudenziana. See **WALK 2**.

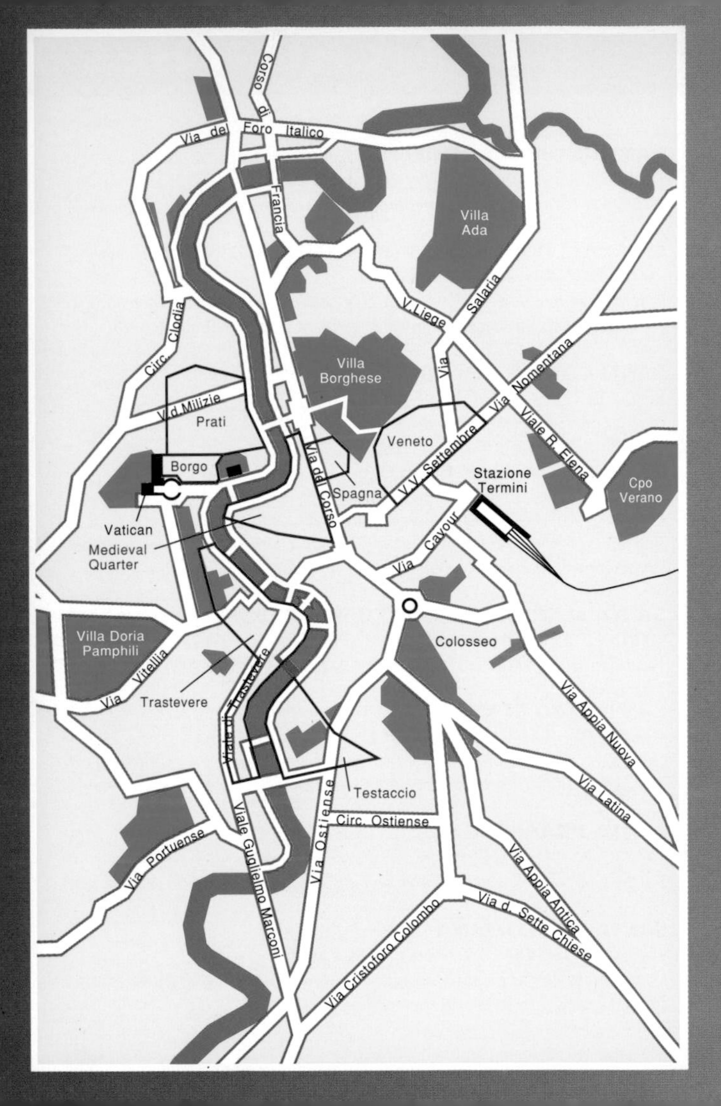
Corso di Francia
Via del Foro Italico
Villa Ada
Salaria
V. Liegi
Circ. Clodia
Villa Borghese
Via
Via Nomentana
V. d. Milizie
Prati
Viale R. Elena
Veneto
Borgo
Via del Corso
V. V. Settembre
Stazione Termini
Spagna
Cpo Verano
Vatican
Via Cavour
Medieval Quarter
Via
Villa Doria Pamphili
Colosseo
Via Vitellia
Trastevere
Via Appia Nuova
Viale di Trastevere
Testaccio
Via Latina
Circ. Ostiense
Via Portuense
Viale Guglielmo Marconi
Via Ostiense
Via Appia Antica
Via d. Sette Chiese
Via Cristoforo Colombo

MEDIEVAL QUARTER Bus 26, 70, 81, 90.
From the Mausoleo di Augusto to the Corso Vittorio Emanuele II, and from the Via del Corso to the Tiber. Narrow, cobblestoned streets, lined with churches and palazzi. *The area also contains the Piazza Navona (see* SQUARES, **A-Z***) and the Pantheon (see* MONUMENTS 1, **A-Z***). See* WALK 4.

SPAGNA M Spagna.
A shoppers' paradise lies beneath the imposing Baroque facade of the Trinità dei Monti church. Indulge yourself in the boutique-lined streets of Via Condotti, Via Mario dei Fiori, Via Bocca di Leone and Via Margutta.

VENETO M Barberini.
From the Via XX Settembre to the Mura Aureliane (see MONUMENTS 3, **A-Z***) and Villa Borghese (see* **A-Z***). The world-famous Via Veneto may be a little out of fashion these days, but it still draws many visitors. The district is home to de luxe hotels, banks, offices, cafés and chic nightclubs.*

TRASTEVERE Bus 56, 60, 75, 170.
On the west bank of the river (the name means 'across the Tiber'), this is one of the oldest and most picturesque areas of the city. See WALK 3, **A-Z**.

TESTACCIO M Piramide.
Monte Testaccio, an ancient artificial hill built of many tons of refuse, pottery chips and rubble from excavations, has given its name to the area lying between the old slaughterhouse, the Piazzale dei Partigiani and the Tiber. An up-and-coming district with many popular trattorias.

PRATI M Lepante/Ottaviano.
A pleasant, middle-class residential area with broad, tree-lined streets, lying between Piazza Cavour, Piazza Risorgimento and Piazza Mazzini.

BORGO M Ottaviano.
Old district between the Vatican City (see **A-Z***) and Castel Sant'Angelo (see* MONUMENTS 1, WALK 4, **A-Z***). Any passage off the Via della Conciliazione will take you into a world of secluded squares (*eg *Piazza delle Vaschette) and narrow, medieval streets (Borgo Pio, Borgo Santo Spirito). See* **A-Z**.

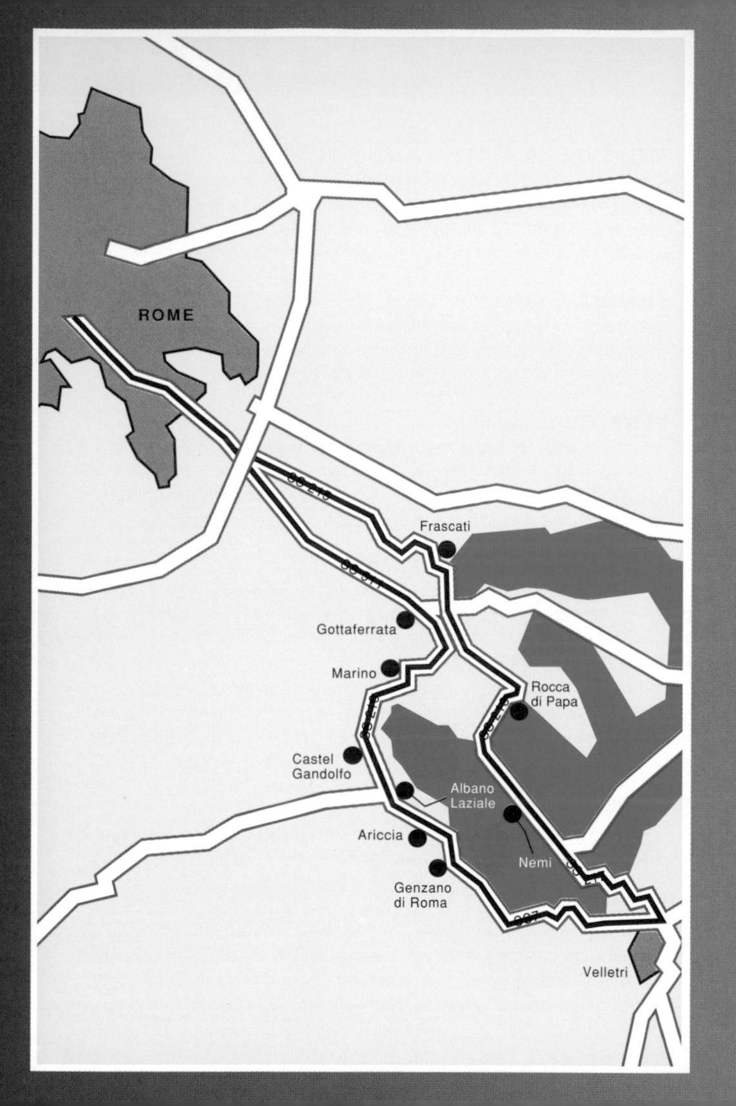
ROME
Frascati
Gottaferrata
Marino
Rocca
di Papa
Castel
Gandolfo
Albano
Laziale
Ariccia
Nemi
Genzano
di Roma
Velletri

Castelli Romani

1 day.

Leave Rome by the Porta San Giovanni and take the SS 215 towards Frascati. At the ring-road (*Raccordo Anulare*), turn right onto the Via Anagnina (SS 511).

27 km - **Grottaferrata**. Immediately after entering the town turn right along the Corso del Popolo to visit the Abbazia di Nilo. The abbey was founded in 1004 by St Nilus, and is the home of Graeco-Catholic Basilian monks who celebrate according to the Greek Orthodox rite. The fortifications were added in the 15thC by Cardinal Giuliano della Rovere, later Pope Julius II. The museum in the forecourt contains illuminated codices, liturgical objects, paintings and enamel-work. In the monastery courtyard is the church of Santa Maria with its beautiful 12thC campanile (bell tower) and a Byzantine-style marble portal. 13thC mosaics adorn the triumphal arch, and the Chapel of St Nilus is decorated with superb frescoes by Domenichino (0900-1200, 1630-1800 daily; museum 0830-1200, 1630-1800 Tues.-Sat., 0830-1000, 1600-1800 Sun.). From the abbey, turn right and then left through the town onto SS 216.

31 km - **Marino**. A beautiful town, with splendid views of Lago Albano and Castel Gandolfo. Admire the town hall, set in the 16thC Palazzo Colonna, and the 17thC church of San Barnaba. The local white wine is delicious, and there is an annual wine festival (*Sagra dell'Uva*) on the first Sunday of October. Follow the road round Lago Albano.

35 km - **Castel Gandolfo** (see **A-Z**). The traditional site of Alba Longa, capital town of the Latin Confederation destroyed by Rome in c.600 BC. The small town is famous today as the Pope's summer residence. Continue along the road which is lined with centuries-old oak trees.

39 km - **Albano Laziale**. This ancient settlement is famous for its white wine, and in summer attracts many thousands of visiting city-dwellers. Emperor Domitian had a luxurious villa here, and Septimius Severus built a fortress and barracks whose cisternone (large water tank) is still working. The town contains much of interest including the fine campanile of the church of S Pietro (12thC), an amphitheatre, and the Tomb of the Horatii and the Curiatii. Leave the town by the Borgo Garibaldi, and cross a 300-m long bridge.

Castel Gandolfo

41 km - **Ariccia**. Visit the lovely Piazza della Repubblica, designed by Bernini (see **A-Z**) in 1665. Continue along the same route.

43 km - **Genzano Di Roma**. Situated on the outer slope of the crater containing Lago di Nemi, this town is famous for the *Infiorata,* a festival of flowers held during the Feast of Corpus Christi (June) when the main street is carpeted with floral illustrations depicting religious themes. Follow the Via Appia Nuova (SS 7) to Velletri.

53 km - **Velletri**. Visit the Cathedral of S Clemente (mostly 14th-15thC), and the Palazzo Comunale (16thC) which houses the municipal museum. Return along the road you came in and turn right following the signs for Rocca di Papa. 8 km further on a road to the left leads to Nemi, a picturesque village which is worth a brief detour. Return to the SS 7and carry on. Then turn right onto the SS 218 to Rocca di Papa. About 1 km before this village, a small road on the right leads to the top of Monte Cavo (950 m), where a hotel-restaurant sits on the site of a temple to Jupiter Laziale, built by Tarquinius Superbus. From here there are excellent views over the lakes and surrounding countryside.

57 km - **Rocca Di Papa**. Small town situated on the northern slopes of Monte Cavo, and surrounded by beautiful countryside. Head downhill to route SS 216, and turn right following the signs for Frascati.

63 km - **Frascati**. This, the most famous of the Castelli Romani, has built its reputation around its fine white wines. It has been popular since Roman times as a holiday resort, and today many rich Roman families keep luxurious villas in the area. There is plenty to see, notably the Cathedral of S Pietro with its magnificent Baroque facade by Girolamo Fontana; the Chiesa del Gesù, a 17thC Jesuit church with a facade attributed to Pietro da Cortona and interior frescoes by Andrea Pozzo; and the 17thC Villa Aldobrandini designed by G. Della Porta. Return to Rome on the Via Tuscolana (SS 215).

Castel Gandolfo

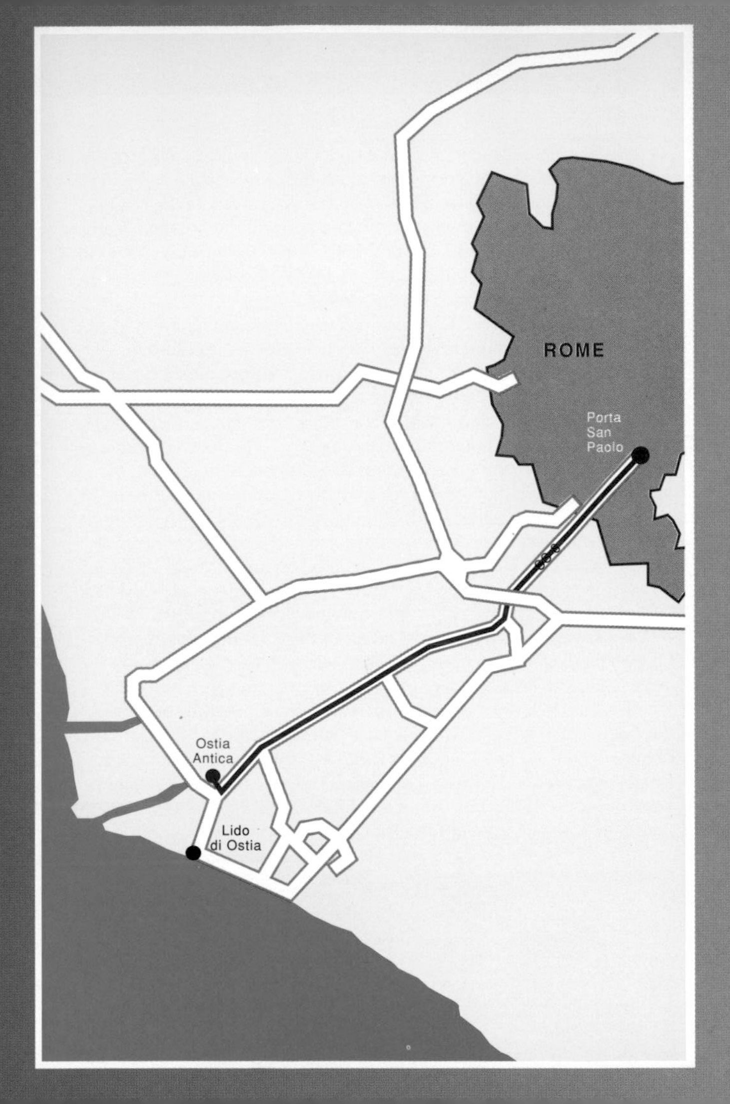
ROME
Porta
San
Paolo
Ostia
Antica
Lido
di Ostia

Ostia Antica

1 day. A trip to visit the ancient ruins of Ostia Antica.

Leave Rome by the Porta San Paolo, and head south west along the Via del Mare (SS 8). After 23 km turn right.
25 km - **Ostia Antica**. The remains of the ancient port of Rome are a must for anyone with an interest in ancient history and archeology. Founded c. 300 BC, it soon became a prosperous trading centre supplying the capital with foodstuffs, and main base of the Roman fleets that helped to conquer the Mediterranean world. The city included a forum, temples, a theatre, public baths, warehouses (*horrea*), and even four- and five-storey apartment blocks (*insulae*). At the height of the Roman Empire it supported a population of over 100,000, but in the 4thC, with the transfer of the Imperial capital to Constantinople by the Emperor Constantine, Ostia fell into decline, and the population gradually abandoned the town to the marshes and their malarial mosquitoes. Since then the sea has receded more than two km, and a great flood in 1575, when the Tiber changed its course, finally buried the remains of the city in sand, helping to preserve most of its archeological treasures to the present day. Excavations during the 19th and 20thCs have revealed a great deal of invaluable evidence concerning day-to-day life in ancient Rome. Works of art recovered from the site are on display in a small museum (*Museo di Ostia*) near the *Casa dei Dipinti* (House of the Painters). Following the Decumanus Maximus (Main Street) from the Porta Romana, you will find: the *Terme di Nettuno* with their floor mosaics, and the well-preserved Via della Fontana which leads to the *Piazzale delle Corporazioni* (Corporations Square), where the merchants' offices were located. Nearby is the theatre, where performances are held in summer. On the right, after the corn warehouses, is the *Casa di Diana*, an apartment block very similar to modern buildings (though the *insulae* were limited to five storeys - 20 m). The *Forum* is dominated by the *Capitolium*, dedicated to Jupiter, Juno and Minerva and close-by is the *Thermopolium* (drinking house). Further west, to the right, is the *Domus di Amore e Psiche* (House of Cupid and Psyche), and opposite are the *Baths of the Seven Sages* (with lavish mosaics). South of the Forum off the Cardo Maximus is the *Domus dei Pesci* (a Christian house) and the *Caupone del Pavone* (Peacock Inn), an ancient wine shop.

ROME
Bagni di Tivoli
TIVOLI
Villa Adriana

Tivoli/Villa Adriana

1 day. Spend the morning exploring the Villa Adriana (take a picnic lunch) and then the afternoon in Tivoli.
Villa Adriana 0900-2000 Tues.-Sun. L. 5000.
Villa d'Este 0900-2000 Tues.-Sun. L. 5000.
Leave Rome by the Via Tiburtina (SS 5).
20 km - Bagni di Tivoli. A spa town whose hot springs, baths, sulphurous waters, and outdoor swimming pools are concentrated in the *Stabilimento delle Acque Albule*. The waters are supposed to have excellent healing properties, but are rather smelly. 3 km beyond the town, a road on the right leads to Hadrian's Villa (Villa Adriana). The vast and sumptuous villa was built in AD 125-134 by Emperor Hadrian (see **A-Z**) on his return from an extensive tour of the Roman Empire. He filled it with the many art treasures he had collected during his trip, and some of the buildings clearly imitate the Hellenic and Egyptian architectural styles which he most admired during his journey. There is a model of the layout of the site in a room beside the café/gift shop which is worth studying before exploring the ruins. Just behind the car park is the colonnaded *Picile* based on the Athenian Stoa Poikile; north east is the *Philosophers' Hall* and *Villa dell'Isola* where the Emperor withdrew for quiet relaxation; in the *Imperial Palace*, some of the floor mosaics in the rooms survive; beyond the large and small baths is the most impressive structure - the *Canopus*, joined to the *Serapeum* buildings modelled on a canal and temple of Serapis from the Nile Valley. Beside the Canopus is a small museum housing recent finds from the excavations. Other statues and items unearthed since the 16thC are scattered in museums throughout the world. Return to the Via Tiburtina, turn right.
35 km - Tivoli. A small town and popular holiday resort for Romans in past centuries. The major attraction here is the Villa d'Este, a former Benedictine convent redesigned by the Neapolitan architect Pirro Ligurio in 1550 for Cardinal Ippolito II d'Este, Governor of Tivoli. You enter through the cloisters of the old monastery. The Old Apartments covered with frescoes lead through to the beautiful terraced gardens filled with magnificent cascading fountains, including: the Avenue of a Hundred Fountains, Oval Fountain, Organ Fountain (*Fontana dell'Organo*) which used to emit a low musical note, Nature Fountain (*Fontana della Natura*), and Dragon Fountain (*Fontana dei Draghi*).

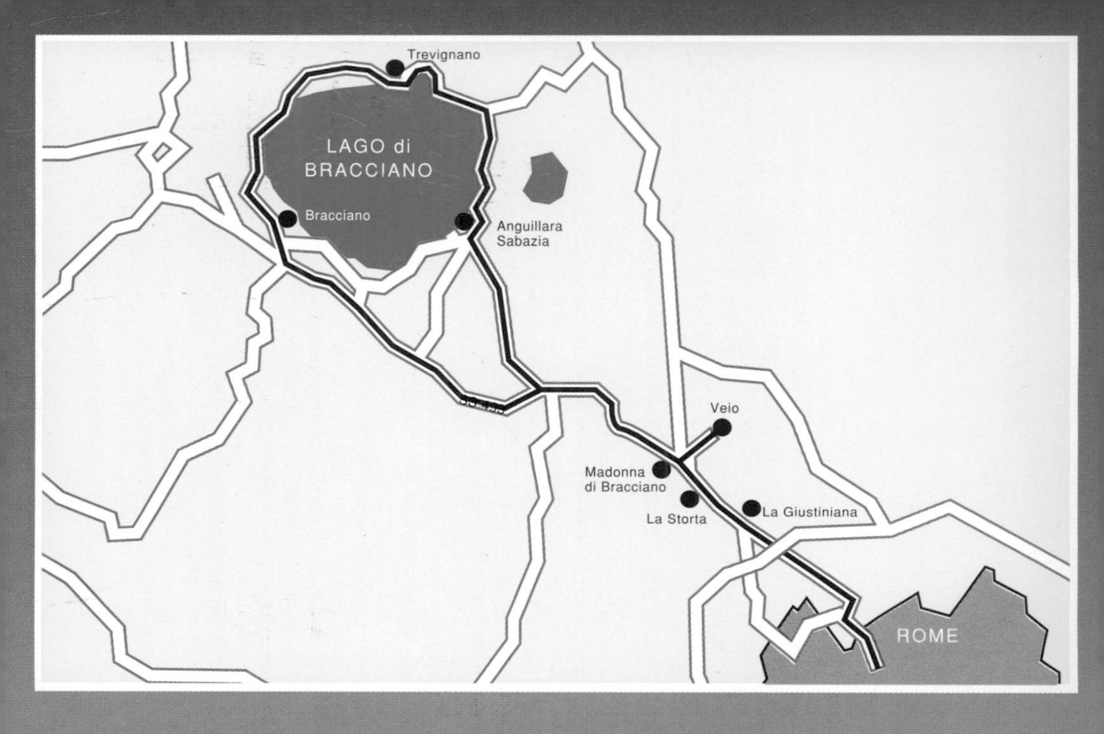
Trevignano
LAGO di
BRACCIANO
Bracciano
Anguillara
Sabazia
Veio
Madonna
di Bracciano
La Storta
La Giustiniana
ROME

Bracciano

1 day.

Leave Rome by the Porta del Popolo travel along the Via Flaminia to the Piazza Appolodoro, take the Corso di Francia to the right, cross the Tiber and branch left into the Via Cassia Nuova. Follow the Via Cassia through La Giustiniana (14 km) and La Storta (17 km) to Madonna di Bracciano (18 km) and branch left again on the Via Claudia to Bracciano.

40 km - **Bracciano**. The imposing Castello Orsini-Odescalchi towers above this delightful town, set on the lush hillside above the Lago di Bracciano. The castle (1485) was associated with the Orsini family until 1696 and is a superb example of Renaissance military architecture. Inside are lavishly decorated rooms (guided tours every hour from 0900-1200, 1500-1700 Tues.-Sat.). The lake is set in an extinct volcanic crater (as are most of the lakes around Rome). There are bathing places and restaurants dotted along the shore, and sailing, motorboats and water-skiing facilities at the various lakeside resorts. From Bracciano follow the lakeside road around to Trevignano.

52 km - **Trevignano**. Visit the fine collegiate church of S Maria Assunta with its 16thC frescoes, and take a stroll along the beach. Continue around the lake to Anguillara Sabazia.

64 km - **Anguillara Sabazia**. A pleasant medieval town set on a basalt promontory overlooking the lake. See the Round Tower in the stronghold above the town, the cobbled street leading up to the church of the Assumption, and the monumental town gate with its clock, or just stroll along the tree-lined lakeside promenade where there is a small beach and harbour. Drive south from Anguillara following the signs for Rome to rejoin the Via Claudia Braccianese (SS 493), continue to the junction with the Via Cassia and turn left (following the signs for Viterbo) then first right to visit Veio.

82 km - **Veio**. The remains of an important Etruscan city, conquered in 396 BC by the Romans after a ten-year siege. See the foundations of the Temple of Apollo, where the famous *Apollo of Veio* was found (now in the Villa Giulia in Rome, see **A-Z**), the frescoes of the Tomba Campana, and the remains of the bathing pool.

Take the Via Cassia back to Rome.

Piramide di Caio Cestio

Foro Romano

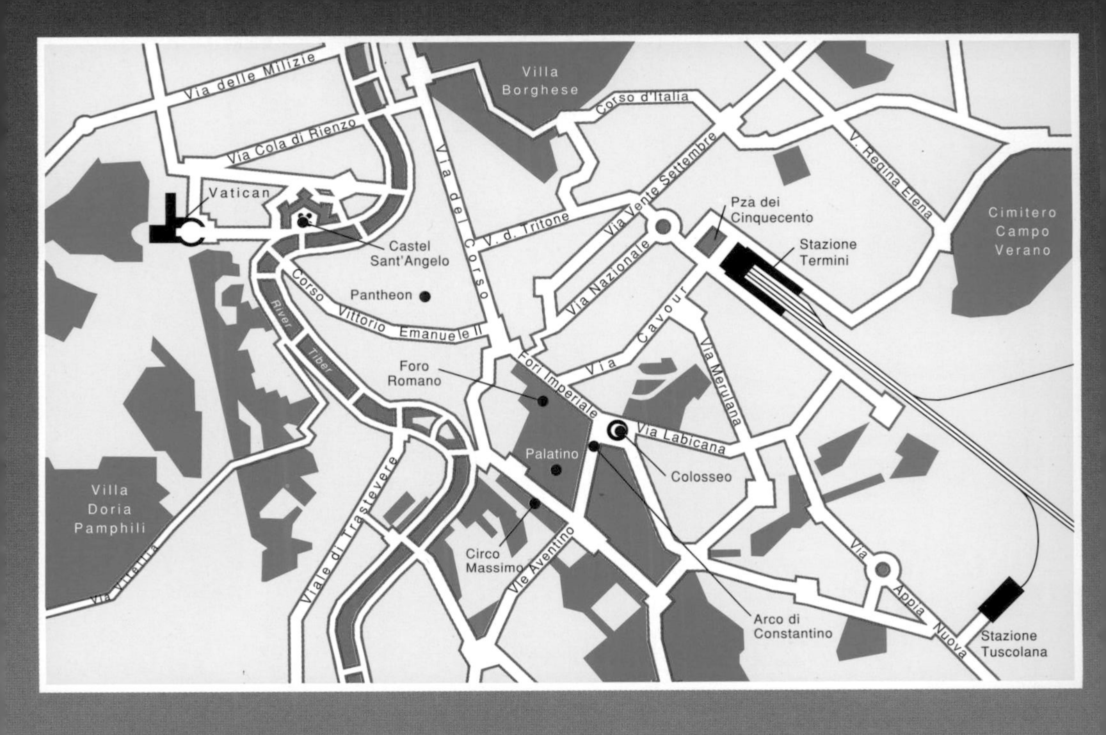

Via delle Milizie
Villa Borghese
Corso d'Italia
Via Cola di Rienzo
V. Regina Elena
Vatican
Via del Corso
Via Vente Settembre
Pza dei Cinquecento
Cimitero Campo Verano
V. d. Tritone
Castel Sant'Angelo
Stazione Termini
Via Nazionale
Pantheon
Corso Vittorio Emanuele II
River Tiber
Via Cavour
Via Merulana
Foro Romano
Fori Imperiale
Via Labicana
Palatino
Colosseo
Villa Doria Pamphili
Viale di Trastevere
Circo Massimo
Vle Aventino
Via Appia Nuova
Via Vitellia
Arco di Constantino
Stazione Tuscolana

COLOSSEO Piazza del Colosseo.
•0900-1900 Mon., Tues., Thurs.-Sat., 0900-1300 Wed., Sun.
M Colosseo. •L. 3000.
The most famous of Rome's ancient monuments. See **WALK 1, A-Z**.

FORO ROMANO Via dei Fori Imperiali.
•0900-dusk Wed.-Sat., 0900-1300 Sun. M Colosseo.
•L. 5000 (including entrance to the Palatino).
The focal point of life in ancient Rome. See **WALK 1, A-Z**.

PALATINO Via di San Gregorio.
•0900-2hrs before sunset Mon.-Sat., 0900-1500 Sun. Closed
Tues. M Colosseo. •L. 5000 (including entrance to Foro Romano).
The cradle of Rome, where legend has it that a she-wolf nursed the infants Romulus and Remus, and site of luxurious imperial villas. See **WALK 1, A-Z**.

ARCO DI CONSTANTINO Piazza del Colosseo.
M Colosseo.
Triumphal arch built in AD 315 to commemorate the Emperor Constantine's (see **A-Z***) victory over Maxentius at the Milvian Bridge. See* **WALK 1, A-Z**.

CIRCO MASSIMO Via del Circo Massimo.
M Circo Massimo.
Huge crowds once gathered here to watch chariot racing and athletics. See **WALK 1, WALK 3, A-Z**.

PANTHEON Piazza della Rotonda.
•0900-1300, 1400-1 hr before sunset Tues.-Sun. Bus 87, 94. •Free.
This magnificent domed building is an architectural masterpiece, and the best-preserved of Rome's ancient monuments. See **WALK 4, A-Z**.

CASTEL SANT'ANGELO Lungotevere Castello.
•0900-1300 Tues.-Sat., 0900-1200 Sun. Bus 64, 280. •L. 3000.
This famous monument has served as a mausoleum, a fortress, a prison and a papal palace, and now houses a museum with military and art collections. See **MUSEUMS 1, WALK 4, A-Z**.

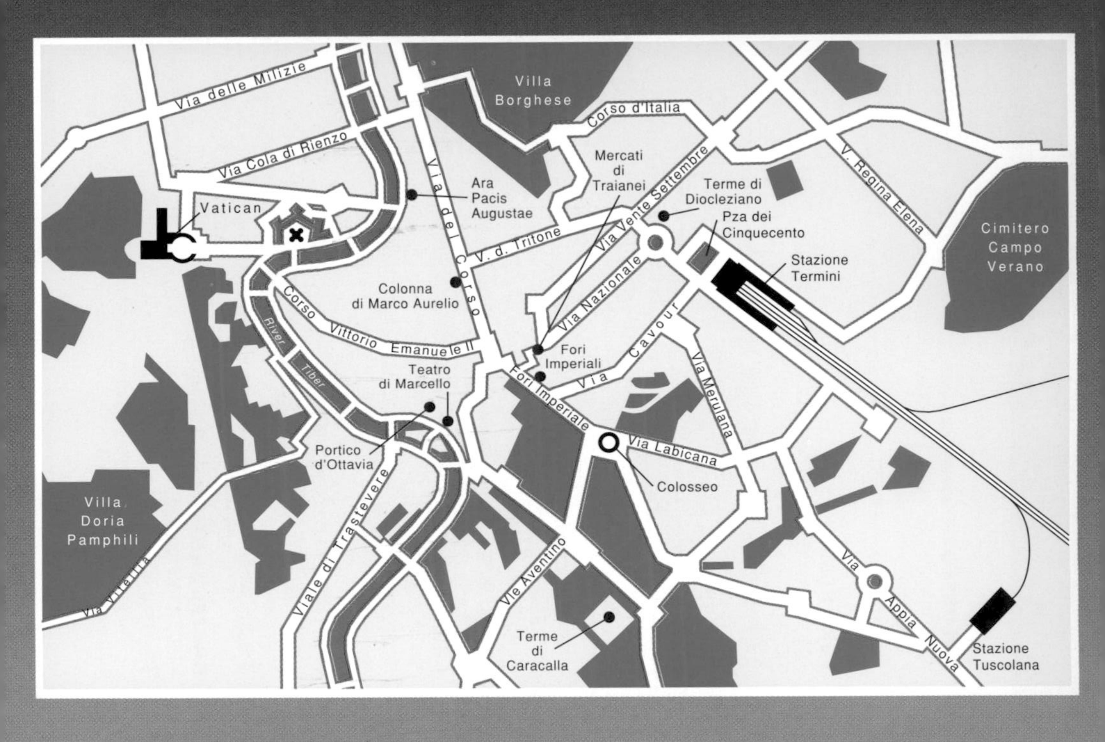
Via delle Milizie
Villa Borghese
Corso d'Italia
Via Cola di Rienzo
Mercati di Traianei
Ara Pacis Augustae
Via Vente Settembre
Terme di Diocleziano
V. Regina Elena
Vatican
Pza dei Cinquecento
Cimitero Campo Verano
V. d. Tritone
Via del Corso
Stazione Termini
Colonna di Marco Aurelio
Via Nazionale
Corso Vittorio Emanuele II
River Tiber
Via Cavour
Fori Imperiali
Via Merulana
Teatro di Marcello
Fori Imperiale
Via Labicana
Portico d'Ottavia
Colosseo
Villa Doria Pamphili
Viale di Trastevere
Vle Aventino
Via Vitellia
Via Appia Nuova
Terme di Caracalla
Stazione Tuscolana

ARA PACIS AUGUSTAE Via di Ripetta.
•0900-1330, 1600-1900 Tues.-Sat., 0900-1300 Sun. M Spagna.
•L. 2000.
Consecrated in 13 BC to celebrate the Pax Romana, following Augustus's (see **A-Z***) victory over Gaul and Spain. See* **A-Z**.

FORI IMPERIALI Via dei Fori Imperiali.
•0900-1300, 1500-1800 Tues.-Sat., 0900-1300 Sun. M Colosseo.
Five separate forums have been excavated here. See **WALK 1**, **A-Z**.

MERCATI DI TRAIANEI Via 4 Novembre.
•0900-1330 Tues.-Sat., (and 1600-1800 Tues., Thurs., Sat.), 0900-1300 Sun. M Colosseo. •L. 2000 (includes entrance to Foro Traiano).
Ancient market by Apollodore of Damascus. See **Fori Imperiali**.

TERME DI DIOCLEZIANO Piazza della Repubblica.
M Repubblica.
The remains of ancient Rome's largest public baths (AD 300). See **A-Z**.

COLONNA DI MARCO AURELIO Piazza Colonna.
M Spagna/Barberini.
Erected AD 180-196 to celebrate the victories of Marcus Aurelius. See **A-Z**.

TEATRO DI MARCELLO Via del Teatro di Marcello.
Bus 57, 90, 116.
Amphitheatre begun by Julius Caesar and completed by Augustus in 11 BC, it now forms part of the Palazzo Orsini. See **WALK 3**, **WALK 4**, **A-Z**.

TERME DI CARACALLA Piazza Numa Pompilio.
•0900-1800 Tues.-Sat., 0900-1300 Sun., Mon. M Circo Massimo.
•L. 3000.
These were the most luxurious baths in ancient Rome. See **A-Z**.

PORTICO D'OTTAVIA Via del Portico d'Ottavia.
Bus 23, 90.
The remains of a portico dedicated by Augustus to his sister. See **WALK 4**.

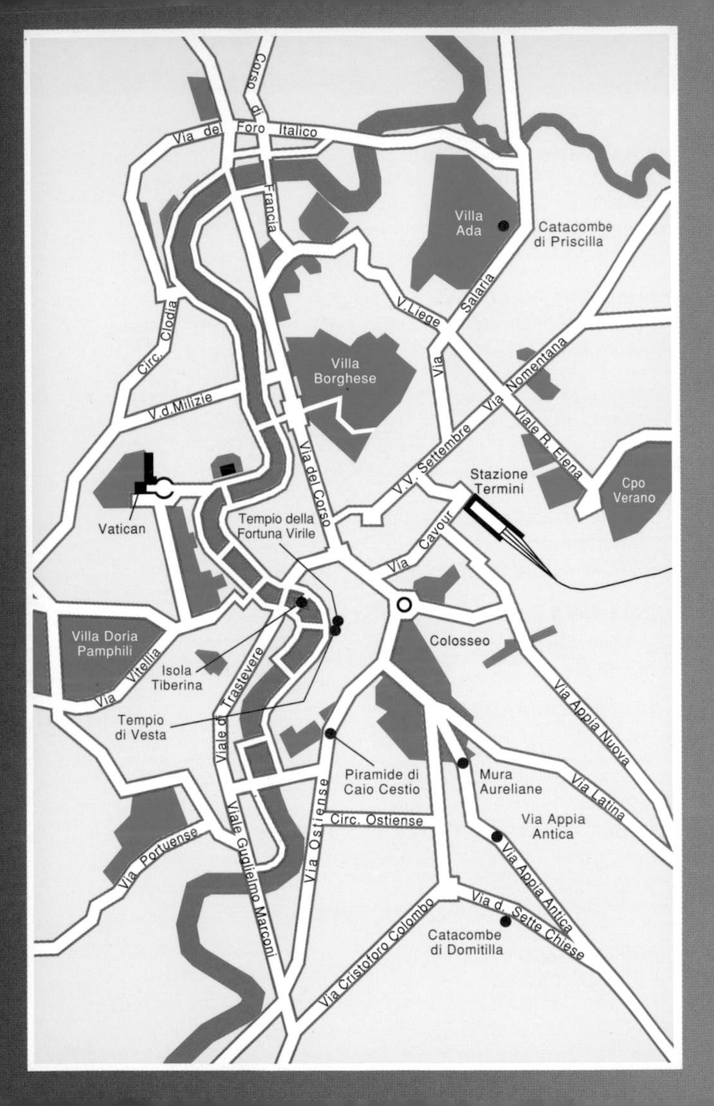
Corso di Francia
Via del Foro Italico
Villa Ada
Catacombe di Priscilla
Via Salaria
V. Liege
Circ. Clodia
Villa Borghese
Via
Via Nomentana
Viale R. Elena
V.d.Milizie
Via del Corso
V.V. Settembre
Stazione Termini
Cpo Verano
Vatican
Tempio della Fortuna Virile
Via Cavour
Villa Doria Pamphili
Via Vitellia
Isola Tiberina
Colosseo
Via Appia Nuova
Tempio di Vesta
Viale di Trastevere
Piramide di Caio Cestio
Mura Aureliane
Via Latina
Via Ostiense
Circ. Ostiense
Via Appia Antica
Via Portuense
Viale Guglielmo Marconi
Via Appia Antica
Via d. Sette Chiese
Catacombe di Domitilla
Via Cristoforo Colombo

ISOLA TIBERINA Ponte Fabricio and Ponte Cestio.
Bus 23, 26.
Site of the Temple of Aesculapius, god of medicine. See **WALK 3**, **A-Z**.

MURA AURELIANE Porta San Sebastiano 18.
•Museo delle Mura 0900-1330 Tues.-Sat. (and 1600-1900 Tues., Thurs.), 0900-1300 Sun. Bus 118 from the Colosseo. •L. 2000.
Massive city wall completed by Emperor Aurelian in AD 279. See **A-Z**.

VIA APPIA ANTICA
Begins from Porta San Sebastiano. Bus 118 from the Colosseo.
The most famous Roman road, linking the city with Brindisi, and originally lined with magnificent monuments and tombs. See **A-Z**.

TEMPIO DELLA FORTUNA VIRILE Piazza Bocca della Verità.
Bus 90, 92, 94, 95.
Elegant Republican temple (2ndC BC). See **WALK 3**, **A-Z**.

TEMPIO DI VESTA Piazza Bocca della Verità.
Bus 90, 92, 94, 95.
Beautiful circular temple dating from the 2ndC BC. See **WALK 3**, **A-Z**.

PIRAMIDE DI CAIO CESTIO Piazza Ostiense.
M Piramide.
The unusual white marble tomb of Caius Cestius, praetor and tribune, who died in 12 BC. See **WALK 3**, **A-Z**.

CATACOMBE DI DOMITILLA Via delle Sette Chiese.
•0830-1200, 1630-1900 Wed.-Mon. Bus 218 from S Giovanni in Laterano. •L. 3000.
The largest catacombs in Rome. See **A-Z**.

CATACOMBE DI PRISCILLA Via Salaria 430.
•0830-1200, 1600-1800 Tues.-Sun. Bus 56 from Piazza Barberini or 57 from Stazione Termini. •L. 3000.
Contains the oldest-known painting of the Virgin and Child (2ndC). See **A-Z**.

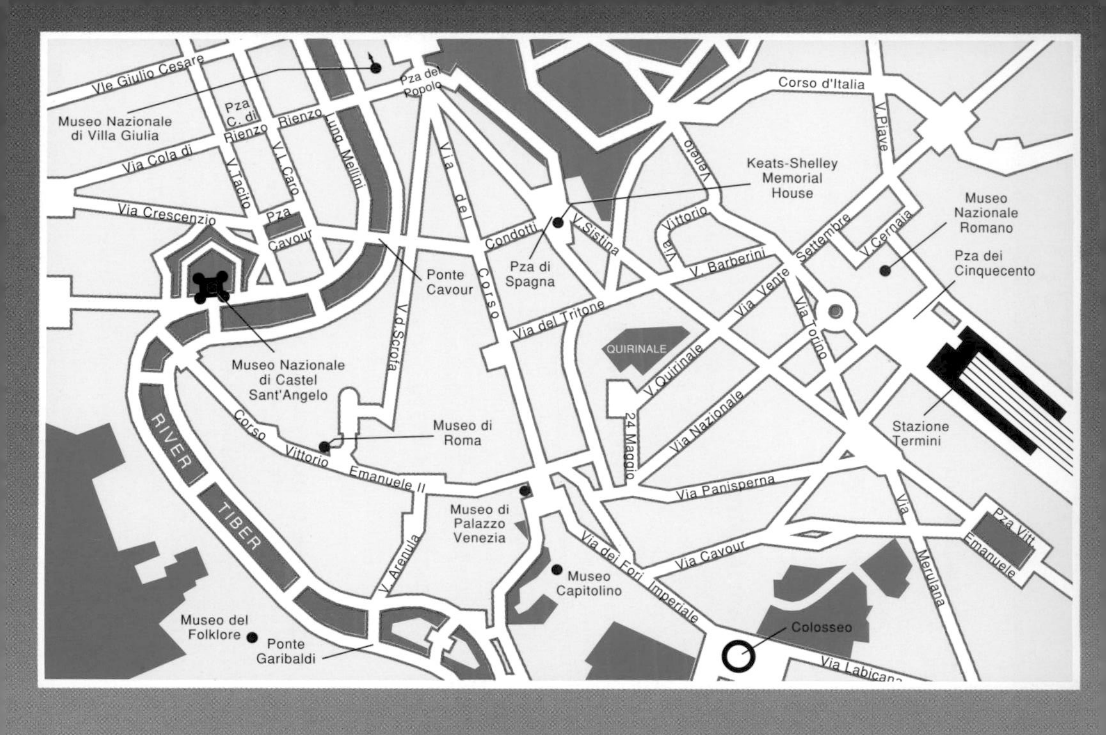

Vle Giulio Cesare
Museo Nazionale
di Villa Giulia
Pza
C. di
Rienzo
Rienzo
Via Cola di
V.Tacito
V.L.Caro
Lung. Mellini
Pza del
Popolo
Via del Corso
Via Crescenzio
Pza
Cavour
Ponte
Cavour
Condotti
Pza di
Spagna
V.Sistina
Keats-Shelley
Memorial
House
Corso d'Italia
V.Piave
Veneto
Via Vittorio
Museo
Nazionale
Romano
Settembre
V.Cernaia
Pza dei
Cinquecento
V. Barberini
Via Vente
Via Torino
Via del Tritone
QUIRINALE
V.Quirinale
Via Nazionale
24 Maggio
Stazione
Termini
V.d.Scrofa
Museo Nazionale
di Castel
Sant'Angelo
Museo di
Roma
Corso
Vittorio
Emanuele II
RIVER
TIBER
Museo di
Palazzo
Venezia
Via Panisperna
Via Merulana
Pza Vitt.
Emanuele
Via Cavour
Via dei Fori Imperiale
Museo
Capitolino
V. Arenula
Museo del
Folklore
Ponte
Garibaldi
Colosseo
Via Labicana

MUSEO CAPITOLINO Piazza del Campidoglio.
•0900-1330 Tues.-Sat. (and 1700-2000 Tues., 2000-2300 Thurs.), 0900-1300 Sun. Bus 26, 87, 90 •L. 4500.
Impressive range of works of art housed in two palazzi. *See* **A-Z**.

MUSEO NAZIONALE ROMANO Piazza dei Cinquecento.
•0900-1400 Tues.-Sat., 0900-1300 Sun. M Repubblica. •L. 4000.
Archeological finds from excavations in and around Rome. See **A-Z**.

MUSEO NAZIONALE DI VILLA GIULIA Ple di Villa Giulia 9.
•0900-1930 Tues.-Sat., 0900-1300 Sun. M Flaminio. •L. 4000.
Superb collection of pre-Roman antiquities. See **Villa Giulia**.

MUSEO NAZIONALE DI CASTEL SANT'ANGELO
Lungotevere Castello.
•0900-1400 Tues.-Sat., 0900-1300 Sun. Bus 23. •L. 3000.
Militaria, paintings, furniture, and tapestries. See **Castel Sant'Angelo**.

MUSEO DI PALAZZO VENEZIA Piazza Venezia 3.
•0900-1400 Mon.-Sat., 0900-1300 Sun. Bus 44, 46, 60, 70, 81.
•L. 4000.
Superb collection of medieval art including 13th-15thC tapestries.

MUSEO DI ROMA Palazzo Braschi, Piazza San Pantaleo 10.
•0900-1400 Tues.-Sat. (and 1700-2000 Wed., Thurs.), 0900-1300 Sun. Bus 46, 62, 64. •L. 3000.
Exhibits illustrating day-to-day life in Rome from 1500 to 1900. See **WALK 4**.

KEATS-SHELLEY MEMORIAL HOUSE Piazza di Spagna 26.
•0900-1300, 1430-1730 Mon.-Fri. M Spagna. •L. 3500.
Keats' house is now a memorial to the two poets who died in Italy. See **A-Z**.

MUSEO DEL FOLKLORE Piazza Sant'Egidio 1B, Trastevere.
•0900-1330 Tues.-Sat. (and 1700-1930 Thurs.), 0900-1200 Sun. Bus 56, 60. •L. 2000.
Dioramas of daily life in Rome during the last two centuries.

Musei Vaticani

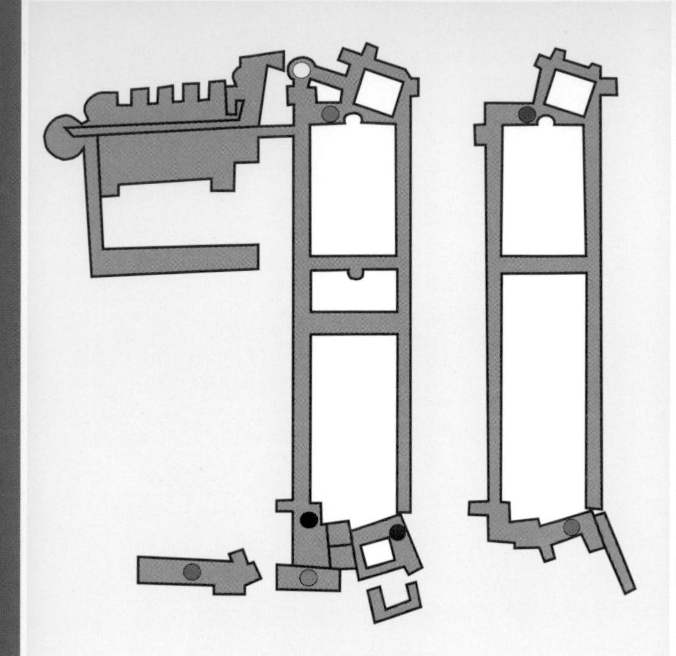

MUSEI VATICANI

- Museo Egizio
- Museo Pio-Clementino
- Museo Etrusco
- Stanze di Raffaello
- Appartamenti Borgia
- Cappella Sistina
- Pinacoteca
- Biblioteca Vaticana

Vatican

MUSEI VATICANI Viale Vaticano, Città del Vaticano.
•0900-1400 Mon.-Fri., 0900-1300 Sat. (0900-1600 Easter, July, Aug., Sept.). Closed on Sun. (except last Sun. of the month when admission is free) and on all religious holidays. M Ottaviano/Bus 64. •L. 8000.
A special bus will take you from the Piazza San Pietro (see **A-Z***) through the Vatican Gardens to the museums, a selection of which are described below. See* **Vatican Museum, A-Z**.

MUSEO EGIZIO
Collection of Egyptian statues, funerary objects and inscriptions.

MUSEO PIO-CLEMENTINO
Founded by Popes Pius VI and Clement XIV in the 18thC, it houses a priceless collection of classical sculpture including the Apollo Belvedere.

MUSEO ETRUSCO
The world's most valuable collection of Etruscan art. Items from the Regolini-Galassi tomb in Room II, and vases and amphorae in Rooms X-XII.

STANZE DI RAFFAELLO
Apartments of Pope Julius II decorated with frescoes by Raphael (see **A-Z***).*

APPARTAMENTI BORGIA
Most notable are the frescoes by Pinturicchio. Room V, the Sala dei Santi *(Room of the Saints), is generally considered to be his best work.*

CAPPELLA SISTINA
Contains The Last Judgement, *the supreme achievement of Michelangelo (see* **A-Z***), as well as the famous ceiling. See* **A-Z**.

PINACOTECA
Large collection of paintings ranging from early Renaissance masters to 19thC religious painters.

BIBLIOTECA VATICANA
Contains over 70,000 codices, manuscripts and early printed books.

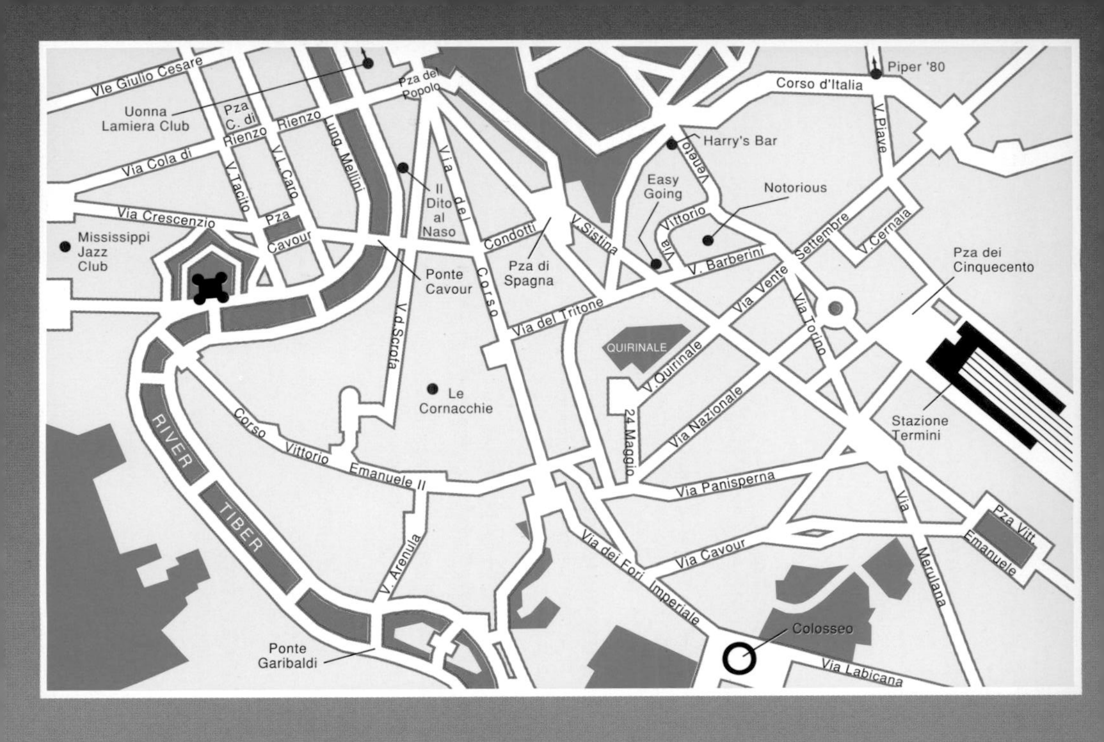
Vle Giulio Cesare
Pza del Popolo
Piper '80
Corso d'Italia
Uonna Lamiera Club
Pza C. di Rienzo
Rienzo
V.Piave
Harry's Bar
Via Cola di
V.L.Caro
Lung. Mellini
Via del
Veneto
Il Dito al Naso
Easy Going
Notorious
V.Tacito
Via Crescenzio
Pza Cavour
Condotti
V. Sistina
Via Vittorio
Settembre
V. Cernaia
Pza dei Cinquecento
Mississippi Jazz Club
Ponte Cavour
Pza di Spagna
V. Barberini
Via Vente
Corso
Via Torino
Via del Tritone
QUIRINALE
V. Quirinale
V.d.Scrofa
Le Cornacchie
Stazione Termini
Via Nazionale
24 Maggio
Corso Vittorio Emanuele II
RIVER TIBER
Via Panisperna
Via
Pza Vitt. Emanuele
Via dei Fori Imperiale
Via Cavour
Merulana
V. Arenula
Colosseo
Ponte Garibaldi
Via Labicana

HARRY'S BAR Via Vittorio Veneto 150.
•1100-0100 Mon.-Sat. M Barberini.
Serves the best cocktails in town. Frequented by journalists and politicians. Restaurant upstairs.

LE CORNACCHIE Via del Pozzo delle Cornacchie 53.
•1300-0200 Wed.-Mon.
Trendy cocktail bar and restaurant with very good music.

IL DITO AL NASO Via del Fiume 4.
•1100-0200 Mon.-Sat. Bus 2, 90.
A private club, but smart dress will guarantee entrance. Once inside you can enjoy excellent cocktails.

NOTORIOUS Via San Nicola da Tolentino 22.
•2230-0330 Tues.-Sun. M Barberini.
Up-market nightspot for the fashionable crowd. Excellent disco.

UONNA LAMIERA CLUB Via Cassia 871.
•2200-0300 daily. Bus 201.
Rock disco featuring New Wave bands and Afro-Caribbean music.

EASY GOING Via della Purificazione 9.
•2230-0330 Tues.-Sun. M Barberini.
Gay disco, but all welcome. One of the liveliest nightspots in town.

MISSISSIPPI JAZZ CLUB Via Aurelia Antica 183, Villa Pamphili (summer), Borgo Angelico 16 (winter).
•1900-0100 Tues.-Sun. Bus 98, 808, 881/M Ottaviano.
Rome's lively jazz venue, featuring many of the top names and best sounds in jazz music.

PIPER '80 Via Tagliamento 9.
•2200-0300 Wed.-Sun. (also 1600-1930 Sat., Sun.). Bus 56.
Popular rock disco, with live bands performing regularly.

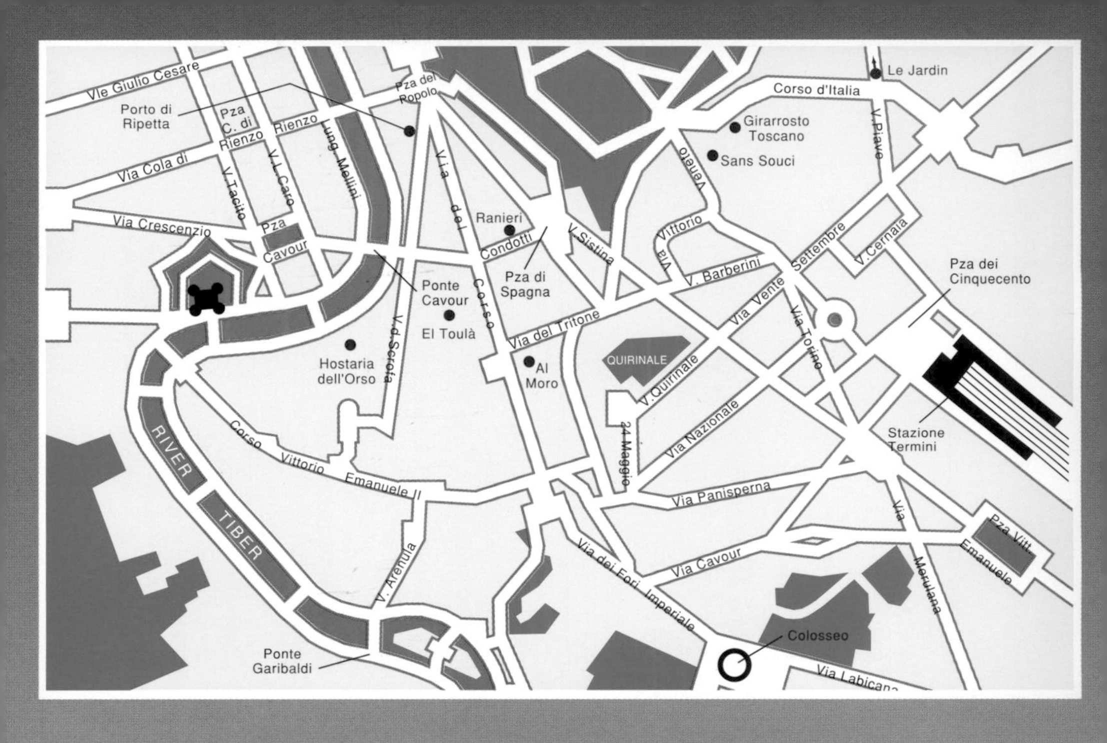

Vle Giulio Cesare
Porto di Ripetta
Pza C. di Rienzo
Rienzo
Via Cola di
V. Tacito
V.L. Caro
Lung. Mellini
Pza del Popolo
Via Crescenzio
Pza Cavour
Via del Corso
Ranieri
Condotti
Pza di Spagna
V. Sistina
Ponte Cavour
El Toulà
V.d. Scrofa
Hostaria dell'Orso
Via del Tritone
Al Moro
QUIRINALE
V. Quirinale
24 Maggio
Via Nazionale
Via Vente
V. Barberini
Via Vittorio
Veneto
Le Jardin
Corso d'Italia
Girarrosto Toscano
Sans Souci
V. Piave
Settembre
V. Cernaia
Via Torino
Pza dei Cinquecento
Stazione Termini
Corso Vittorio Emanuele II
RIVER TIBER
V. Arenula
Ponte Garibaldi
Via Panisperna
Via Cavour
Via dei Fori Imperiale
Via Merulana
Pza Vitt. Emanuele
Colosseo
Via Labicana

Expensive

SANS SOUCI Via Sicilia 20.
•2000-0200 Tues.-Sun. Closed Aug. M Barberini.
Luxurious, high-class restaurant. Haute cuisine served until late.

EL TOULÀ Via della Lupa 29b.
•1200-1500, 2000-2300 Mon.-Sat. Closed Sat. lunchtime, Sun. Bus 81, 90.
Considered by many to be the best restaurant in Rome, El Toulà offers delicious Veneto *(Venetian) specialities in sumptuous surroundings.*

HOSTARIA DELL'ORSO Via del Soldati 25.
•1930-2400 Mon.-Sat. Bus 26, 70, 81, 87, 90.
Set in a magnificent 13thC palazzo. *Also piano-bar and a nightclub.*

RANIERI Via Mario dei Fiori 26.
•1230-1500, 1930-2300 Mon.-Sat. Closed Mon. lunchtime. M Spagna.
Offers fine, traditional Italian cooking in an old-world atmosphere.

GIRARROSTO TOSCANO Via Campania 29.
•1200-1500, 2000-2400 Tues.-Sun. Closed Aug. Bus 118.
In the cellar of a palazzo *facing the Mura Aureliane. Tuscan specialities.*

PORTO DI RIPETTA Via di Ripetta 250.
•1200-1500, 2000-0030 Mon.-Sat. Bus 2, 90.
Inventive meat and fish dishes for a discerning clientele.

AL MORO Vicolo delle Bollette 13.
•1230-1500, 2000-2300 Mon.-Sat. Closed Aug. M Barberini.
Delicious Roman food in a pleasant and lively setting near to the Fontana di Trevi. The waiters have a reputation as the most arrogant in the city.

LE JARDIN Via G. de Notaris 5, Parioli.
•1200-1500, 2000-2400 Mon.-Sat. Closed 10-20 Aug. M Flaminio.
In the fashionable Lord Byron Hotel and one of the best restaurants in Italy. Refined French and Italian cuisine.

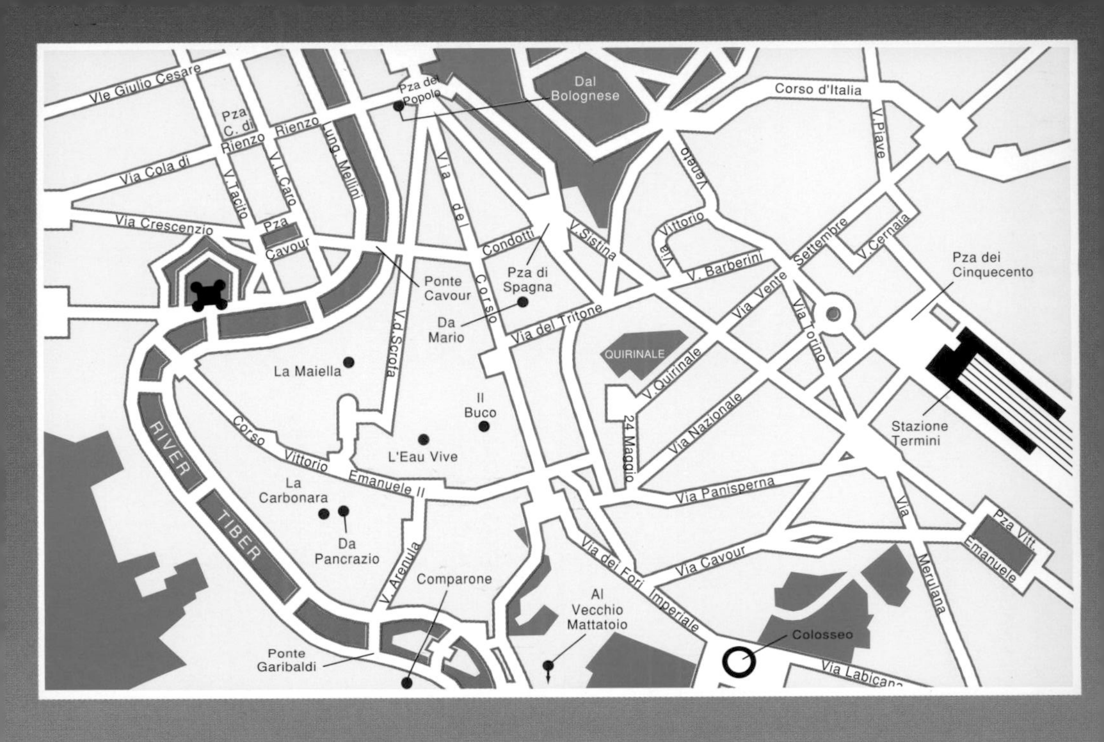
Vle Giulio Cesare
Pza del Popolo
Dal Bolognese
Corso d'Italia
V.Piave
Pza C. di Rienzo
Rienzo
Lung. Mellini
Via Cola di
V.Tacito
V.L.Caro
Via del Corso
Veneto
Via Vittorio
Via Crescenzio
Pza Cavour
Condotti
V.Sistina
V. Barberini
Settembre
V.Cernaia
Pza dei Cinquecento
Ponte Cavour
Pza di Spagna
Via Vente
Via Torino
Da Mario
V.d.Scrofa
Via del Tritone
QUIRINALE
V.Quirinale
La Maiella
Il Buco
Via Nazionale
Stazione Termini
24 Maggio
Corso Vittorio Emanuele II
L'Eau Vive
RIVER TIBER
La Carbonara
Da Pancrazio
Via Panisperna
Via Merulana
Pza Vitt. Emanuele
V. Arenula
Comparone
Via dei Fori Imperiale
Via Cavour
Al Vecchio Mattatoio
Ponte Garibaldi
Colosseo
Via Labicana

Moderate

DA PANCRAZIO Piazza del Biscione 92-94.
•1200-1500, 1900-2400 Thurs.-Tues. Bus 60, 64.
Occupies the site of the ancient Teatro di Pompeo, where Cicero says that Julius Caesar's murder took place. Excellent Italian cuisine.

LA CARBONARA Piazza Campo dei Fiori 23.
•1200-1500, 2000-2300 Wed.-Mon. Closed 12-22 Aug. Bus 62, 64.
Traditional Roman cooking. Superb variety of pasta, fresh fish and desserts.

DAL BOLOGNESE Piazza del Popolo 1-2.
•1200-1500, 2000-2300 Mon.-Fri. Closed 5-21 Aug. M Flaminio.
Home-made pasta and Bolognese specialities attract a fashionable crowd.

IL BUCO Via di Sant'Ignazio 8.
•1200-1500, 2000-2300 Tues.-Sun. Closed 15-31 Aug. Bus 64.
Small, charming restaurant serving traditional Florentine cuisine.

AL VECCHIO MATTATOIO Piazza O. Giustiniani 2, Testaccio.
•1200-1500, 2000-2400 Wed.-Mon. Bus 27, 92.
Friendly atmosphere and traditional Roman-style dishes.

DA MARIO Via delle Vite 55.
•1200-1500, 2000-2300 Mon.-Sat. Closed 5-30 Aug. M Spagna.
Tuscan specialities include game (in season) and cannellini *(white beans).*

LA MAIELLA Piazza Sant'Apollinare 45-46.
•1200-1500, 2000-2400 Mon.-Sat. Bus 26, 90, 91.
Excellent trattoria in medieval setting. Specialities from the Abruzzo district.

COMPARONE Piazza in Piscinula 47, Trastevere.
•1200-1500, 2000-2300 Tues.-Sun. Bus 23, 56, 60.
Pleasant spot serving genuine Roman grilled fish and meat dishes.

L'EAU VIVE Via Monterone 85.
•1200-1500, 1900-2300 Mon.-Sat. Closed 21 July-28 Aug. Bus 64.
Unusual restaurant run by nuns in a 16thC palazzo *built for Pope Leo X.*

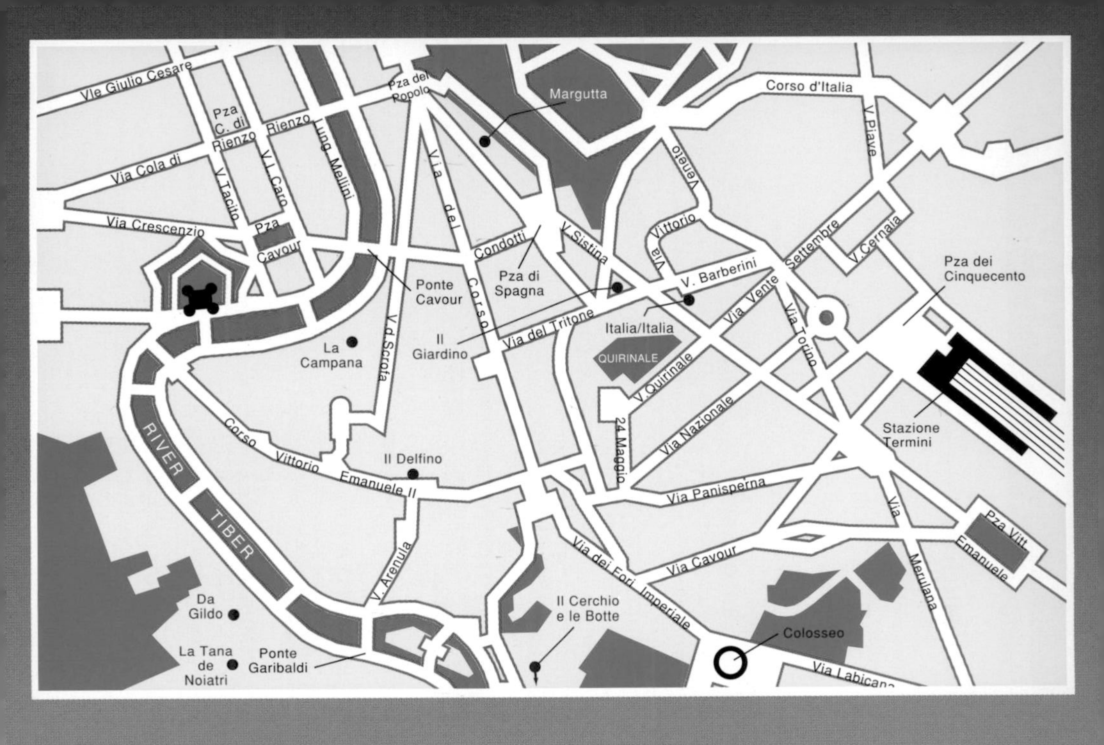

Vle Giulio Cesare
Pza del Popolo
Margutta
Corso d'Italia
V. Piave
Pza C. di Rienzo
Rienzo
Lung. Mellini
Via Cola di
V. Tacito
V. L. Caro
Via del Corso
Veneto
Via Vittorio
Via Crescenzio
Pza Cavour
Condotti
Pza di Spagna
V. Sistina
Settembre
V. Cernaia
Pza dei Cinquecento
V. Barberini
Via Vente
Ponte Cavour
Il Giardino
Via del Tritone
Italia/Italia
Via Torino
QUIRINALE
La Campana
V. d. Scrofa
V. Quirinale
Via Nazionale
24 Maggio
Stazione Termini
RIVER TIBER
Corso Vittorio Emanuele II
Il Delfino
Via Panisperna
Via Merulana
Pza Vitt. Emanuele
Via Cavour
Via dei Fori Imperiale
V. Arenula
Il Cerchio e le Botte
Da Gildo
La Tana de Noiatri
Ponte Garibaldi
Colosseo
Via Labicana

Budget

LA CAMPANA Vicolo della Campana 18.
• 1200-1500, 2000-2400 Tues.-Sun. Closed Aug. Bus 81, 90
Good cocktails and delicious Roman cooking in this eating-house dating back to the 16thC. Try the Alicette gratinate *(anchovies au gratin).*

DA GILDO Via della Scala 13a.
• 1230-1530, 1930-0130 Mon.-Sat. Bus 23, 28, 65.
High-quality pizzeria.

MARGUTTA Via Margutta 119.
• 1200-1500, 1800-2300 Tues.-Sun. M Spagna.
Pleasant vegetarian restaurant, set in the fashionable shopping area near Piazza di Spagna (see SQUARES, **A-Z***).*

IL CERCHIO E LE BOTTE Via Luca della Robbia 15.
• 1200-1500, 2000-0100 Mon.-Sat. Bus 27.
Simple Roman trattoria *in the popular Testaccio district (see* CITY DISTRICTS*) serving large helpings of good, wholesome food.*

LA TANA DE NOIANTRI Via della Paglia 13.
• 1200-1500, 2000-2300 Wed.-Mon. Bus 44, 56, 60.
Named after the local festival of Noiantri *(see* **Events***) held in Trastevere (see* CITY DISTRICTS, **A-Z***). Traditional Roman food in a simple setting.*

IL GIARDINO Via Zucchelli 29.
• 1200-1500, 2000-2400 Tues.-Sun. Closed Aug. M Barberini.
Simple, good value Roman cooking. Try to get a table in the little garden.

ITALIA/ITALIA Via Barberini 2-16.
• 1100-0100 Wed.-Mon. M Barberini.
Large fast-food restaurant serving pasta, burgers, pizzas and ice-cream.

IL DELFINO Corso Vittorio Emanuele II 67.
• 1200-1500, 1900-2300 Tues.-Sun. Closed Aug. Bus 26, 64, 81.
Small restaurant with tavola calda *(hot buffet), salad bar, and take-away counter. The roast chicken is recommended.*

Dept Stores/Markets

COIN Piazzale Appio.
•0900-2000 Tues.-Sat. Closed Mon. a.m. M San Giovanni.
Rome's top department store. Five floors of clothes, household goods and electrical appliances. Good value for money.

LA RINASCENTE Piazza Colonna & Piazza Fiume.
•0900-2000 Tues.-Sat. Closed Mon. a.m. M Barberini.
The Piazza Colonna branch sells clothes, perfume, fashion accessories and toys, while the Piazza Fiume branch specializes in household goods.

STANDA Viale Trastevere 60 & Via Cola di Rienzo 173.
•0900-2000 Tues.-Sat. Closed Mon. a.m. Bus 56, 60, 90, 95.
Inexpensive household goods. The Via Cola di Rienzo branch has a fine food department.

UPIM Via del Tritone 172 & Via Nazionale 211.
•0900-2000 Tues.-Sat. Closed Mon. a.m. M Barberini.
This chain store features very cheap clothing and household goods.

CAMPO DEI FIORI Piazza Campo dei Fiori.
•0600-1400 Mon.-Sat. Bus 26, 62, 64, 90.
Lively market selling fresh fruit and vegetables, fish, delicatessen, flowers, and even some second-hand clothes. See WALK 4, A-Z.

PIAZZA VITTORIO EMANUELE II Piazza Vittorio Emanuele II.
•0700-1400 Mon.-Sat. M Termini.
Rome's biggest street market for anything from fancy pasta to cheap shoes.

MERCATO DEI FIORI Via Trionfale/Via Paolo Sarpi.
•1000-1300 Tues. M Ottaviano then Bus 70.
Flower market. Makes a good starting point for a walk in the Prati district (see CITY DISTRICTS*).*

VIA SANNIO Via Sannio.
•0800-1300 Mon.-Fri., 0800-1900 Sat. M San Giovanni.
Second-hand clothes and accessories.

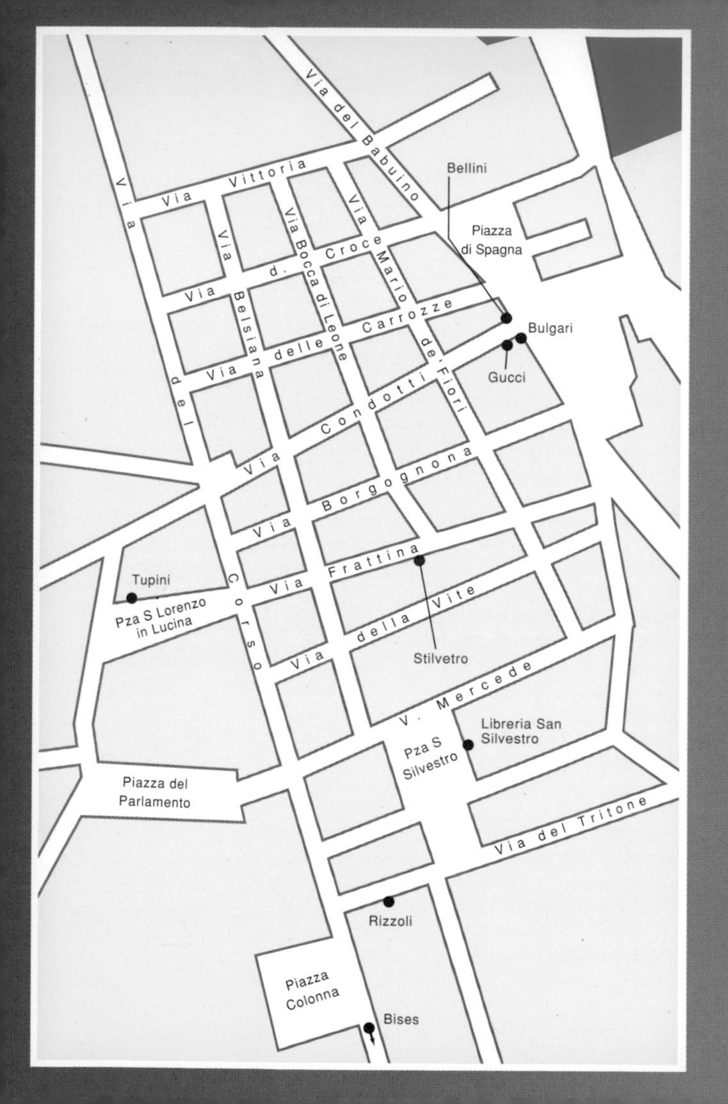

Via del Babuino
Via Vittoria
Via del Corso
Via d. Croce
Via Belsiana
Via Bocca di Leone
Via Mario de' Fiori
Via delle Carrozze
Bellini
Piazza di Spagna
Bulgari
Gucci
Via Condotti
Via Borgognona
Via Frattina
Via della Vite
Tupini
Pza S Lorenzo in Lucina
Corso
Stilvetro
V. Mercede
Libreria San Silvestro
Pza S Silvestro
Piazza del Parlamento
Via del Tritone
Rizzoli
Piazza Colonna
Bises

Gifts

RIZZOLI Galleria Colonna at Largo Chigi 15.
•1000-1300, 1530-1930 Tues.-Sat. Closed Mon. a.m. Bus 56, 81, 90.
The largest bookshop in Italy, catering for a wide variety of tastes.

LIBRERIA SAN SILVESTRO Piazza San Silvestro 27.
•1000-1300, 1530-1930 Tues.-Sat. Closed Mon. a.m. Bus 56, 81, 90.
Bookshop with an excellent arts department. Many bargains.

BULGARI Via Condotti 10.
•1000-1300, 1530-1930 Tues.-Sat. Closed Mon. a.m. M Spagna.
A white marble facade advertises one of the world's greatest jewellers.

GUCCI Via Condotti 8 & 76-77.
•1000-1300, 1530-1930 Tues.-Sat. Closed Mon. a.m. M Spagna.
World-famous range of clothes, luggage, bags, belts and shoes.

BISES Via del Gesù 93.
•1000-1300, 1530-1930 Tues.-Sat. Closed Mon. a.m.
Bus 26, 64, 81, 90.
Wonderful collection of luxurious fabrics, set in a 17thC palace.

BELLINI Piazza di Spagna 77.
•1000-1300, 1530-1930 Tues.-Sat. Closed Mon. a.m. M Spagna.
Exquisite, expensive, hand-embroidered table linen, sheets, etc.

TUPINI Piazza San Lorenzo in Lucina 8.
•1000-1300, 1530-1930 Tues.-Sat. Closed Mon. a.m. M Spagna.
Specializes in chinaware, but also sells beautiful crystal and silverware.

STILVETRO
Via Frattina 56.
•1000-1300, 1530-1930 Tues.-Sat. Closed Mon. a.m. M Spagna.
Good value Italian tableware and glassware.

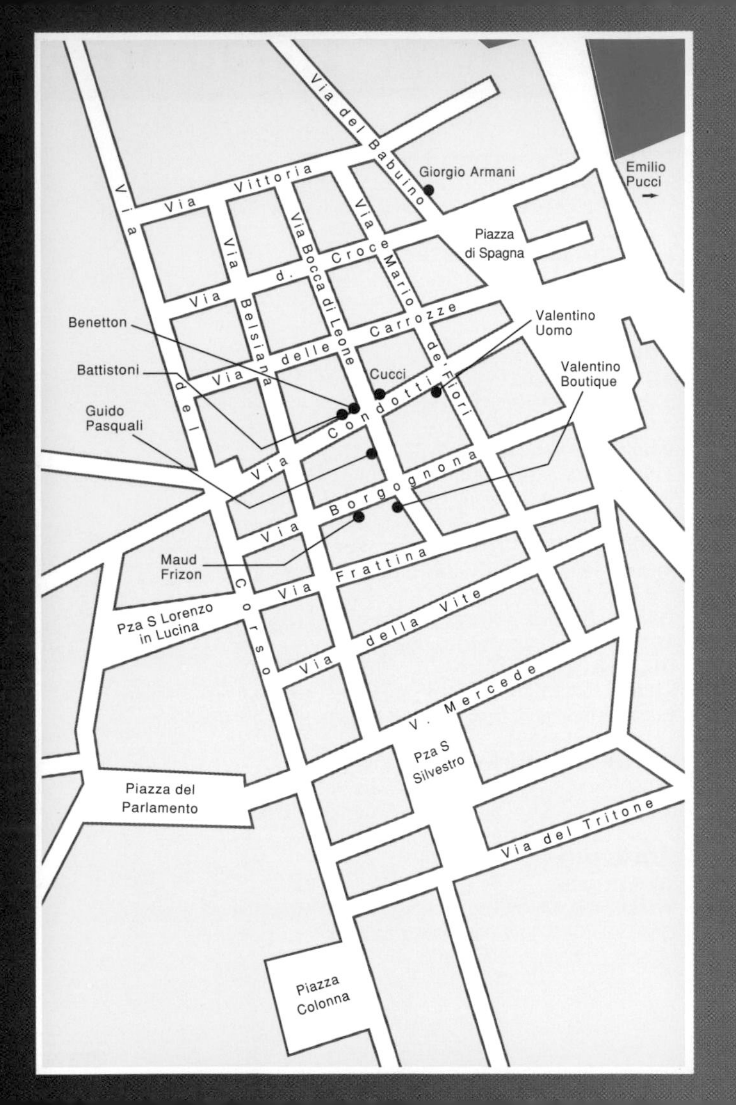

Via del Babuino
Giorgio Armani
Emilio Pucci
Via Vittoria
Via
Via Bocca di Leone
Via Mario de' Fiori
Via d. Croce
Piazza di Spagna
Via Belsiana
Via delle Carrozze
Benetton
Valentino Uomo
Battistoni
Cucci
Valentino Boutique
Guido Pasquali
Via Condotti
Via Borgognona
Maud Frizon
Via Frattina
Via del Corso
Pza S Lorenzo in Lucina
Via della Vite
V. Mercede
Pza S Silvestro
Piazza del Parlamento
Via del Tritone
Piazza Colonna

Fashion

CUCCI Via Condotti 67.
•1000-1300, 1530-1930 Tues.-Sat. Closed Mon. a.m. M Spagna.
Expensive, top-quality menswear.

BATTISTONI Via Condotti 57.
•1000-1300, 1530-1930 Tues.-Sat. Closed Mon. a.m. M Spagna.
Classic Italian fashion for men.

VALENTINO UOMO Via Mario dé Fiori 22.
•1000-1300, 1530-1930 Tues.-Sat. Closed Mon. a.m. M Spagna.
Exquisitely tailored suits and shirts for men. Also belts and accessories.

EMILIO PUCCI Via Campania 59.
•1000-1300, 1530-1930 Tues.-Sat. Closed Mon. a.m. Bus 56.
Ready-to-wear clothes from the most famous of Florentine designers.

GIORGIO ARMANI Via del Babuino 102.
•1000-1300, 1530-1930 Tues.-Sat. Closed Mon. a.m. M Spagna.
Inventive fashion from the talented Milanese designer.

BENETTON Via Condotti 59.
•1000-1930 Mon.-Sat. M Spagna.
Pullovers galore - all sizes, shapes and colours, in wool and in cotton.

VALENTINO BOUTIQUE Via Bocca di Leone 15-18.
•1000-1300, 1530-1930 Tues.-Sat. Closed Mon. a.m. M Spagna.
Rome's leading designer provides high fashion for the younger woman.

MAUD FRIZON
Via Borgognona 38.
•1000-1300, 1530-1930 Tues.-Sat. Closed Mon. a.m. M Spagna.
The queen of Paris shoe designers. Very expensive, Italian-made footwear.

GUIDO PASQUALI Via Bocca di Leone 5.
•1000-1300, 1530-1930 Tues.-Sat. Closed Mon. a.m. M Spagna.
A shoe designer of great originality, at eminently affordable prices.

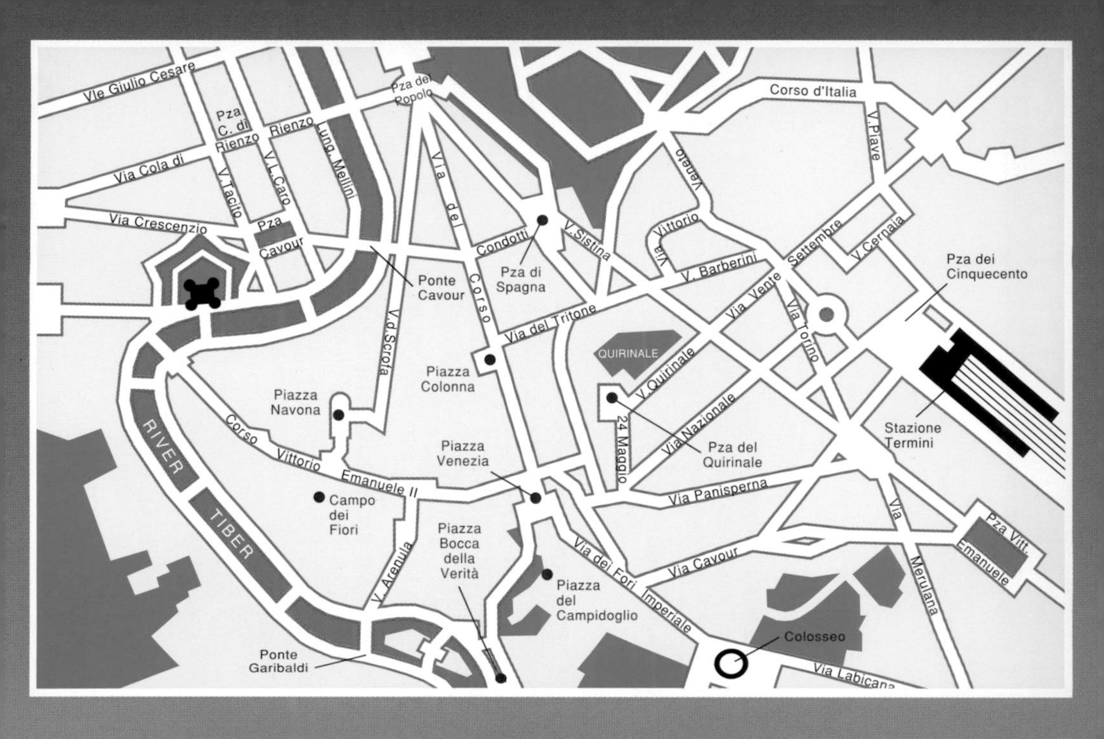
Vle Giulio Cesare
Pza del Popolo
Corso d'Italia
V.Piave
Pza C. di Rienzo
Rienzo
Lung. Mellini
Via Cola di
V.L.Caro
V.Tacito
Veneto
Via Crescenzio
Pza Cavour
Via del Corso
Condotti
Pza di Spagna
V.Sistina
Via Vittorio
Settembre
V.Cernaia
Pza dei Cinquecento
Ponte Cavour
V. Barberini
Via Vente
Via Torino
Via del Tritone
QUIRINALE
V.Quirinale
Stazione Termini
V.d.Scrofa
Piazza Colonna
Piazza Navona
Via Nazionale
Pza del Quirinale
24 Maggio
Corso Vittorio Emanuele II
Piazza Venezia
Via Panisperna
RIVER TIBER
Campo dei Fiori
Piazza Bocca della Verità
Via dei Fori Imperiale
Via Cavour
Via Merulana
Pza Vitt. Emanuele
V. Arenula
Piazza del Campidoglio
Colosseo
Ponte Garibaldi
Via Labicana

PIAZZA DI SPAGNA M Spagna.
One of the most popular tourist spots in the city, the Spanish Steps being one of the principal attractions. See **A-Z**.

PIAZZA NAVONA Bus 26, 70, 81, 90.
Beautiful oval piazza in the heart of the Medieval Quarter. See **WALK 4**, **A-Z**.

PIAZZA DEL POPOLO M Flaminia.
French-style piazza *completed in 1820 by Valadier, set at the foot of the Pincio (see* **A-Z**). *Features the oldest obelisk in Rome. See* **A-Z**.

PIAZZA DEL CAMPIDOGLIO M Colosseo.
Impressive square, designed by Michelangelo (see **A-Z**), *flanked by the Museo Capitolino (see* **MUSEUMS 1**, **A-Z**) *and the church of Santa Maria in Aracoeli (see* **CHURCHES 2**, **A-Z**). *See* **WALK 4**, **A-Z**.

PIAZZA DEL QUIRINALE M Barberini/Repubblica.
Facing the Presidential palace, this square offers one of the best panoramas in the city.

PIAZZA COLONNA M Barberini.
A lively square, beneath the palazzi Chigi *and* Wedekind, *and featuring the Colonna di Marco Aurelio (see* **MONUMENTS 2**, **A-Z**).

CAMPO DEI FIORI Bus 26, 62, 64, 90.
One of the most pleasant squares in Rome, surrounded by charming old buildings, and featuring an attractive market. See **SHOPPING 1**, **WALK 4**, **A-Z**.

PIAZZA BOCCA DELLA VERITÀ M Colosseo.
A picturesque square on the site of Foro Boario (the cattle-market of ancient Rome), beneath the lovely facade of S Maria in Cosmedin (see **CHURCHES 2**, **A-Z**). *See* **WALK 3**, **A-Z**.

PIAZZA VENEZIA Bus 64.
*Dominated by the controversial Monumento a Vittorio Emanuele II (***WALK 4**, **A-Z**). *A busy and congested traffic junction. See* **WALK 1**, **WALK 4**.

Ancient Rome

All day. Take a picnic lunch.

Begin at M Circo Massimo. Turn right out of the Metro and into the Piazza di Porta Capena. Ahead on the left is the large area of grassland which was once the site of the biggest race-course in the Ancient World - the Circo Massimo (see **MONUMENTS 1**, **A-Z**). Cross the square and head along Via di S Gregorio towards the Arco di Constantino visible in the distance (see **MONUMENTS 1**, **A-Z**). About half-way along on the left is the monumental gateway which leads onto the Palatino (see **A-Z**). Take the steps to the left and follow the path which crosses the remains of Nero's aqueduct and climbs past the Domus Severiana to the Stadio Domiziano (96-81 BC). Cross the top of the stadium, and continue through the Domus Augustana (the imperial apartments), the Antiquarium (an ancient convent, now used to store archeological finds), and the Domus Flavia, with its courtyard and octagonal fountain, to reach the Casa di Livia. Nearby is the Criptoportico, the semi-underground corridor linking the imperial apartments, supposedly the spot where Caligula was ambushed and assassinated in AD 41. Walk up to the Orti Farnesiani (Farnese Gardens), ideal for a picnic lunch among the pine-trees, and admire the excellent views over the Tiber and the Vatican (see **A-Z**), and down to the Foro Romano (see **MONUMENTS 1**, **A-Z**) and the Colosseo (see **MONUMENTS 1**, **A-Z**). Afterwards, walk down the Clivus Palatinus, past the Arco di Tito, towards the church of Santa Maria Romana. On the right is the Antiquarium Forense, which exhibits archeological finds, mostly from the Tempio di Vesta and the Basilica Aemilia. Turn left along the Via Sacra. On the right is the Basilica of Maxentius with its three imposing arches, and just beyond that is the Tempio di Romolo (4thC), and behind it the church of Santi Cosma e Damiano (see **CHURCHES 3**). Bear left to the circular Tempio di Vesta and the neighbouring Atrium Vestae. The atrium is still visible, with pools surrounded by statues. Continue along the Via Sacra past the three Corinthian columns of the Tempio di Castore e Polluce (484 BC) on the left and along past the Basilica Giulia, built by Julius Caesar (see **A-Z**) in 50 BC. Ahead is the Tempio di Saturno, with its eight rough columns, and up to the left the twelve columns of the Portico degli Dei Consenti. Turn right past the Colonna di Phoca

Foro Romano

Arco di Tito, Foro Romano

(Column of Phocas) on the right to the Arco di Settimo Severo, erected in AD 203. To the right down some steps is the Lapis Niger, a black marble stone bearing an obscure inscription, traditionally thought to mark the tomb of Romulus. Ahead is the stern brick facade of the Curia, which once housed the Roman Senate, and to the left of the Arch is the Rostri (Imperial Rostra), or orators' platform. From the Curia, turn right past the Basilica Aemilia, then left between this and the Tempio di Antonio e Faustina (AD 141), and leave the Forum by the exit onto the Via della Salara Vecchia. Turn left past the church of S Luca e Martina, through the Foro di Cesare (separated from the other forums by the Via dei Fori Imperiali), to the Piazza Venezia (see **SQUARES**), then right around the Colonna di Traiano (see **A-Z**) to reach the steps leading to Via IV Novembre and the Foro di Traiano (see **Fori Imperiali**). Beyond the 13thC Torre delle Milizie turn right into the Salita del Grillo, past the Foro di Augusto (see **Fori Imperiali**), and continue down Via Tor di Conti, across Via Cavour and along Via del Colosseo to the Largo Agnesi and the steps down to the Colosseo (see **MONUMENTS 1**, **A-Z**).

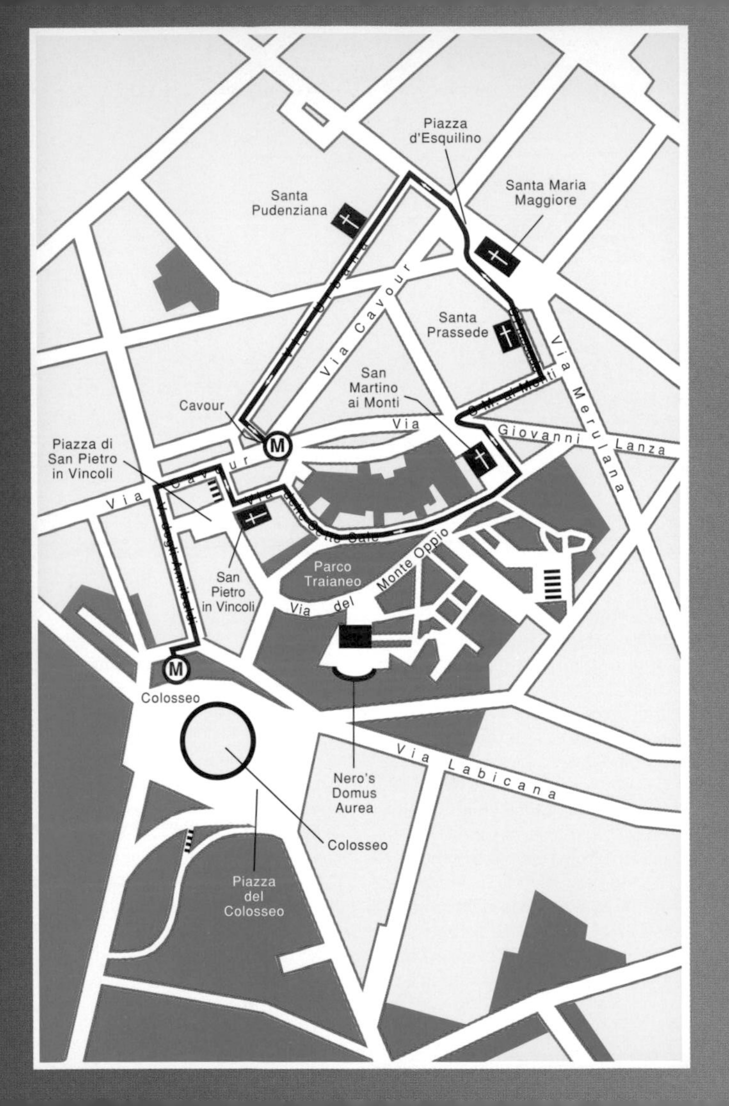
Piazza d'Esquilino
Santa Maria Maggiore
Santa Pudenziana
Via Cavour
Santa Prassede
Via Merulana
San Martino ai Monti
Cavour
Via Giovanni Lanza
Piazza di San Pietro in Vincoli
Via Cavour
San Pietro in Vincoli
Parco Traianeo
Via del Monte Oppio
Colosseo
Via Labicana
Nero's Domus Aurea
Colosseo
Piazza del Colosseo

Esquilino

2hr 30 min.

Begin at M Colosseo. From the metro, climb the flight of steps on the left up to the Largo Agnesi. Follow the Via degli Annibaldi straight ahead, then turn right into the Via Cavour. 100 m along, at Via di S Francesco di Paola, steps lead right under the Palazzo Borgia to the Piazza di San Pietro in Vincoli with its restored 5thC church (see **CHURCHES 3**, **A-Z**). This houses the chains which bound St Peter in Jerusalem, and also the magnificent *Moses* by Michelangelo (see **A-Z**). Enter the narrow Via delle Sette Sale on your right as you leave the church and follow it past the Parco Traianeo (with the Domus Aurea visible beyond - see **Nero**) until it merges with the Via del Monte Oppio. A little further ahead, on the left, stands the Baroque facade of San Martino di Monti, designed by Gagliardi. The original building dates from c. 500 (replacing a 4thC foundation) and was rebuilt in the 9thC. Turn left out of the church into the Via Equizia, cross the Via Giovanni Lanza and then turn right into the Via di San Martino ai Monti, then turn left down the Via di Santa Prassede. Just before you reach the main road you come to the 7thC church of Santa Prassede (see **CHURCHES 3**), famous for its magnificent 9thC mosaics. Leave the church by the side door, and go left to the basilica of Santa Maria Maggiore (see **CHURCHES 1**, **A-Z**). The interior is breathtaking, and its campanile (75 m) is the highest in Rome. After visiting the basilica, cross the Piazza d'Esquilino. The obelisk in the centre is one of two which originally stood at the entrance to the Mausoleo di Augusto (see **A-Z**); the other stands in the Piazza del Quirinale (see **SQUARES**). Cross the Via Cavour and turn left into the Via Urbana. On the right is the 19thC facade of Santa Pudenziana (see **CHURCHES 3**). The original church dates from the 5thC, and is one of the oldest in the city. It was built on the site of a house which belonged to a Roman citizen named Pudens, who once gave sanctuary to St Peter. The church is dedicated to his daughter Pudenziana, and the church of Santa Prassede is dedicated to her sister. The beautifully restored mosaics in the apse depict Christ seated on a golden throne surrounded by his Apostles and the two sisters.
Continue along Via Urbana to finish the walk at M Cavour.

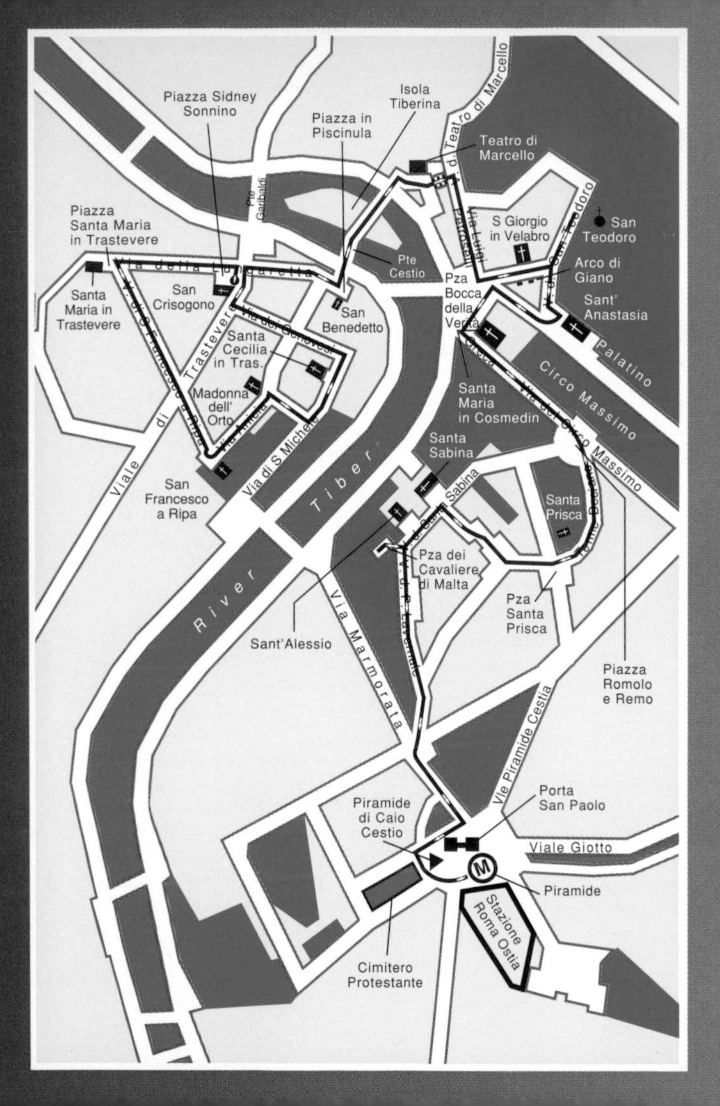

Piazza Sidney Sonnino
Isola Tiberina
Piazza in Piscinula
V. d. Teatro di Marcello
Teatro di Marcello
Pte Garibaldi
Piazza Santa Maria in Trastevere
Via della Lungaretta
Pte Cestio
Via Luigi Petroselli
S Giorgio in Velabro
San Teodoro
V. d. San Teodoro
Arco di Giano
Santa Maria in Trastevere
San Crisogono
Trastevere
Via dei Genovesi
San Benedetto
Pza Bocca della Verità
Sant' Anastasia
Santa Cecilia in Tras.
Madonna dell' Orto
Via Anicia
V. di S Francesco a Ripa
Viale di Trastevere
Palatino
Circo Massimo
Via del Circo Massimo
Santa Maria in Cosmedin
Greca
Santa Sabina
Via di S Michele
San Francesco a Ripa
River Tiber
Santa Prisca
Pza dei Cavaliere di Malta
Pza Santa Prisca
Sant'Alessio
Via Marmorata
Piazza Romolo e Remo
Vle Piramide Cestia
Porta San Paolo
Piramide di Caio Cestio
Viale Giotto
M
Piramide
Stazione Roma Ostia
Cimitero Protestante

Trastevere - Aventino

4-5 hours.

Begin in Piazza Sidney Sonnino in Trastevere (see **CITY DISTRICTS**, **A-Z**). The church of San Crisogono stands on the *piazza*, a monumental 12thC building which sits on top of the remains of a 5thC church. Follow the Via della Lungaretta to Piazza Santa Maria in Trastevere. Its church was the first to be dedicated to the Virgin Mary (3rdC) and the present building dates from the 12thC (see **CHURCHES 1**). Go along the Via di San Francesco a Ripa across the busy Viale di Trastevere to the church of San Francesco a Ripa. Inside, in the fourth chapel to the left, is the beautiful statue of the Blessed Louisa Bertoni (1674), by Bernini (see **A-Z**). On your right as you leave the church the Via Anicia leads to the lovely church of Madonna dell'Orto (Our Lady of the Orchard), whose interior is extravagantly decorated on the theme of fruits and flowers. Go down the street opposite, to Via di San Michele, and turn left to reach the imposing tower of Santa Cecilia in Trastevere (see **CHURCHES 2**). Turn left into Via dei Genovesi to Via Trastevere, right across Piazza Sidney Sonnino, and right again into Via della Lungaretta, which leads to Piazza in Piscinula and the pretty little church of San Benedetto. Bear left up a small flight of steps towards the Ponte Cestio which leads across the river to Isola Tiberina (see **MONUMENTS 3**, **A-Z**), with the Roman campanile and Baroque facade of San Bartolomeo. Continue across the Ponte Fabricio on the other side of the island, to the Teatro di Marcello (see **MONUMENTS 2**, **A-Z**). Climb down the steps to the right of the *teatro*, walk across and up to Via del Teatro di Marcello and along Via Luigi Petroselli (on the right is the Foro Boario). Turn left across the street to Piazza Bocca della Verità (see **SQUARES**). Turn left and pass by the ancient Arco di Giano (Arch of Janus). To the left is the simple facade of San Giorgio in Velabro, with a Roman portico and campanile. Inside are some beautiful 13thC frescoes by Pietro Cavallini. Turn left into Via di San Teodoro to see the attractively restored, 6thC circular church of San Teodoro, and return to the far end of the street where, on the left, is the pleasing facade of Sant'Anastasia, designed by Bernini. Turn right to return to the Piazza Bocca della Verità. On the left is the church of Santa Maria in Cosmedin (see **CHURCHES 2**, **A-Z**) whose Romanesque campanile overlooks the well-

Santa Maria in Trastevere

Piazza Santa Maria in Trastevere

S Maria in Cosmedin

preserved Tempio di Vesta (see **MONUMENTS 3**, **A-Z**) and Tempio della Fortuna Virile (see **MONUMENTS 3**, **A-Z**) across the way. Turn left into Via della Greca and then Via del Circo Massimo to reach Piazzale Romolo e Remo, which offers broad views over the Circo Massimo (see **MONUMENTS 1**, **A-Z**) and across to the Palatino (see **A-Z**). Cross the square and follow the curving Via delle Terme Deciane, then turn right into Piazza Santa Prisca. The church (up the steps to the right) has been restored, but it sits on a very ancient site. Cross the square and head towards the summit of the Aventino, along the Via del Tempio di Diana until you reach the magnificent 5thC church of Santa Sabina (5thC). There are excellent views over the Tiber from the terraced garden beside the church. Continue right along Via di Santa Sabina, past Sant'Alessio (rather poorly renovated during the 18thC), to the lovely Piazza dei Cavalieri di Malta (Square of the Knights of Malta), designed by the 18thC engraver Piranesi. The artist is buried in the small church in the gardens of the Priorata di Malta (No. 3), residence of the Grand Master of the Knights of Malta. A unique view of the dome of St Peter's (see **CHURCHES 1**, **San Pietro in Vaticano**) may be had by peering through the keyhole of the priory gate. Head downhill on the Via di Porta Lavernale and Via Marmorata to the white marble Piramide di Caio Cestio (see **MONUMENTS 3**, **A-Z**) and the Porta San Paolo (see **A-Z**). Behind the pyramid is the Cimitero Protestante (see **A-Z**), a romantic spot well worth a visit before finishing your walk at M Piramide.

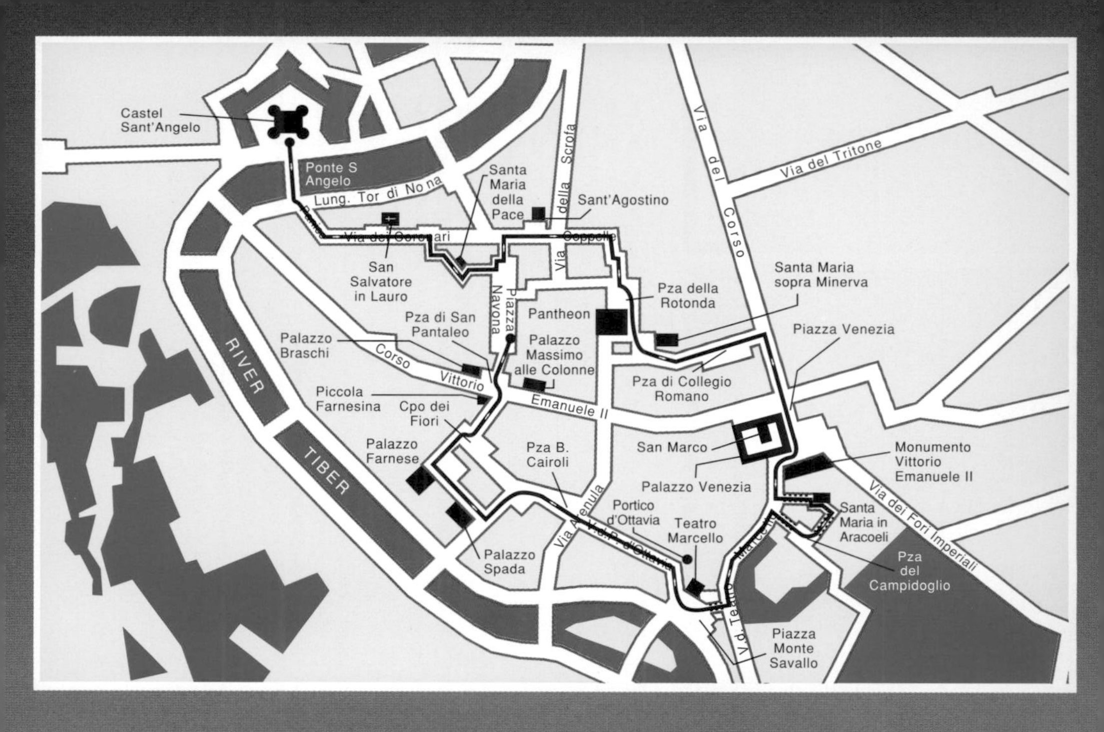

Castel Sant'Angelo
Ponte S Angelo
Lung. Tor di Nona
Santa Maria della Pace
Sant'Agostino
Via della Scrofa
Via dei Coronari
Via Coppelle
San Salvatore in Lauro
Piazza Navona
Pza della Rotonda
Santa Maria sopra Minerva
Via del Corso
Via del Tritone
Pantheon
Pza di San Pantaleo
Palazzo Braschi
Corso Vittorio Emanuele II
Palazzo Massimo alle Colonne
Piazza Venezia
Pza di Collegio Romano
Piccola Farnesina
Cpo dei Fiori
RIVER
TIBER
Palazzo Farnese
Pza B. Cairoli
San Marco
Monumento Vittorio Emanuele II
Palazzo Venezia
Via dei Fori Imperiali
Via Arenula
Portico d'Ottavia
Teatro Marcello
Santa Maria in Aracoeli
Palazzo Spada
Pza del Campidoglio
Piazza Monte Savallo
V.d. Teatro

Renaissance Palaces & Churches

4-5 hours.

Begin with a visit to the Castel Sant'Angelo (see **MONUMENTS 1**, **A-Z**), then cross Ponte Sant'Angelo (see **A-Z**), and fork left into the Via di Panico and left again into the Via dei Coronari. This street was laid out in the late 15thC by Pope Sixtus IV, to bring light and fresh air into this congested area. Today it is lined with antique dealers and other specialist shops. Along on the left is San Salvatore in Lauro which has a lovely Renaissance cloister. Further along (opposite the Piazzetta di S Simeone) turn right into Vicolo di Montevecchio to the *piazza* and *palazzo* of the same name. Raphael (see **A-Z**) had a studio here. Head down into the Via Arco della Pace and then left, which leads you to the church of Santa Maria della Pace, with a facade by Pietro da Cortona. The church contains frescoes by Raphael (*The Sybils*), and by Baldassare Peruzzi, and to its left is an elegant cloister by Donato Bramante (see **A-Z**). Across and to the left is Vicolo della Pace which leads to the rear of Santa Maria dell'Anima (German Catholic church), topped by an interesting campanile whose roof is covered in multi-coloured earthenware tiles. Go around the church and across the Via dell'Anima into the Via di Lorenesi and onto the Piazza Navona (see **SQUARES**, **A-Z**). Turn left and left again into the Via Agonale, and then right through the archway and down the Via di S Agostino to reach the square and church of Sant'Agostino. The church is early Renaissance, but was somewhat insensitively restored in the 18th and 19thCs. It contains some masterpieces, notably the *Madonna del Parto* by Sansovino (just inside to the left), *The Prophet Isaiah* by Raphael, and the *Pilgrim's Madonna* by Caravaggio (see **A-Z**), in the first chapel to the left. Cross the Via della Scrofa, along the Via delle Coppelle, then right into the Via della Maddalena and the Via del Panteone to the Piazza della Rotonda, which is overlooked by the impressive facade of the Pantheon (see **MONUMENTS 1**, **A-Z**). Follow, to its left, the Via della Minerva to the Gothic church of Santa Maria sopra Minerva (see **CHURCHES 2**). Inside, don't miss the frescoes by Filippino Lippi, and the fine 15thC wooden *Crucifixion* in the innermost right-hand chapel. On the *piazza* outside stands a small marble elephant bearing an obelisk, by Bernini (see **A-Z**). Now take the Via Pie di Marmo, Piazza di Collegio Romano,

Monumento a Vittorio Emanuele II

and turn right into the Via del Corso to the Piazza Venezia (see SQUARES). Next, bear right across the square to visit the church of San Marco, part of the Palazzo Venezia (see **A-Z**). Inside is a Cosmatesque floor, an 11thC mosaic in the apse, and the *San Marco Evangelista* by Melozzo da Forli in the sacristy. Cross the Piazza di San Marco and walk a little way up the Via del Teatro Marcello beside the imposing Monumento a Vittorio Emanuele II (see **A-Z**), then left up the steps to the unusual brick facade of Santa Maria in Aracoeli (see **CHURCHES 2**, **A-Z**). Just to its right are steps leading to the majestic Piazza del Campidoglio (see **SQUARES**, **A-Z**). Descend to the Via del Teatro Marcello, turn left down the hill past the remaining three Corinthian columns of the Temple of Apollo Sosianus (5thC BC), and turn right, down the steps and up into the Piazza Monte Savallo in front of the Teatro di Marcello (see **MONUMENTS 2**, **A-Z**). Enter the former Jewish Quarter (Ghetto) along the Via del Portico d'Ottavia past the ruins of the Portico d'Ottavia, which once boasted 300 columns (see **MONUMENTS 2**). This is an ancient and very picturesque district where for centuries the Jewish community was confined under Papal orders. Continue into the Via di S Maria del Pianto, cross the busy Via Arenula into the Piazza Benedetto Cairoli and then bear right into the Via dei Giubbonari, left (opposite Largo Dei Librari) into the Via Arco del Monte, and right into the Via di Capo di Ferro. Ahead, in the Piazza Capo di Ferro, is the Palazzo Spada (see **ART GALLERIES**, **A-Z**), built in 1540 and restored by Borromini (see **A-Z**). A little further along the Via Capo di Ferro you will find the Palazzo Farnese (see **A-Z**) which houses the French Embassy. Cross the Piazza Campo dei Fiori (see **SHOPPING 1**, **SQUARES**, **A-Z**) and head through the Via dei Baulari. On the left, facing the Piazza di San Pantaleo, is the Piccola Farnesina which houses the Museo Baracco (see **A-Z**), temporarily closed to the public at the time of writing. To the left is the Palazzo della Cancelleria, built between 1483 and 1517 by Bramante, and belonging to the Vatican (see **A-Z**). Ahead are the Palazzo Braschi, which houses the Museo di Roma (see **MUSEUMS 1**) and, further along the Corso Vittorio Emanuele II on the left, is the Palazzo Massimo alle Colonne. Follow the Via Cuccagna between these last two to end your walk back in the peaceful setting of the Piazza Navona (see **SQUARES**, **A-Z**).

Accidents and Breakdowns: In the event of an accident follow the usual procedure of exchanging names, addresses and insurance details. To contact the police or other emergency services, tel: 113 (see **Emergencies**). If someone is injured and you are held responsible insist on contacting your consulate (see **A-Z**) as soon as possible. Breakdowns: A red warning triangle should be placed 50 m behind your vehicle. Tel: 116 for the ACI (Automobile Club d'Italia). There are emergency telephones at 1 km intervals along motorways. Press the red button for medical assistance and the green button for the breakdown service. See **Driving**.

Accommodation: There are countless hotels and *pensioni* (guest houses) in Rome. Hotels are rated from de luxe and 1st to 4th class and *pensioni* from P1 to P3. Prices range from about L. 60,000 for a double room with a bath in the cheapest categories to L. 100,000/L. 150,000 for mid-priced hotels and *pensioni*, to L. 500,000 or more in de luxe hotels. By law, prices are displayed on the door of the room, and are usually exclusive of breakfast, but should include service and taxes. The peak season is April-October but the demand is high all year round, especially for medium-priced establishments in the historic centre around the Pantheon (see MONUMENTS 1, WALK 4, **A-Z**), Piazza Navona (see SQUARES, WALK 4, **A-Z**) and Piazza Campo dei Fiori (see SHOPPING 1, SQUARES, WALK 4, **A-Z**), so booking is essential to ensure good quality and a decent area. There are many cheap establishments around Stazione Termini (see **Railways**), but the area is rather drab. Luxury accommodation is concentrated around the Via Veneto (see CITY DISTRICTS), Villa Borghese (see **A-Z**), Spagna (see CITY DISTRICTS) and Barberini. A day hotel (*albergo diurno*) at the station rents rooms by the hour to allow travellers to freshen up, but sleeping facilities are not provided. The EPT (see **Tourist Information**) provide accommodation advice and a list of hotels. Their offices at Stazione Termini, Fiumicino (see **Airports**) and at the main motorway entrances to the city also have a free booking service. See **Camping and Caravanning**, **Youth Hostels**.

Airports: Leonardo da Vinci (Fiumicino), 36 km south west of Rome, handles the bulk of international and domestic flights (tel: 60121).

Facilities include toilets, restaurants, bars, accommodation, shops, car rental, *etc.* There is a bus service to Stazione Termini (see **Railways**) every 15 min (it takes about one hour and costs L. 5000). Taxis are faster but expensive (approx. L. 40,000 to the city centre). Ciampino Airport, 16 km south of Rome on the Via Appia Nuova, handles mainly charter flights (tel: 4694). It has all the usual facilities and there is a bus service to Stazione Termini every 30 min (approx. 30 min journey, costs L. 2800). A taxi will cost approx. L. 25,000.

Ara Pacis Augustae: This altar in the Via di Ripetta is one of the best-preserved monuments of ancient Rome. It was consecrated in the year 13 BC to celebrate the Pax Romana following the victory of Augustus (see **A-Z**) over Spain and Gaul. The screen surrounding the altar is richly decorated with reliefs of foliage and animals, and sculptured historical and mythological scenes. See **MONUMENTS 2**.

Arco di Constantino: A triumphal arch dedicated to the Emperor Constantine (see **A-Z**) by the Senate and the Roman people in AD 315 after his victory over Maxentius at the Ponte Milvio, in the north of the city. Many of its decorative elements, such as the frieze over the central arch, came from other monuments. See **MONUMENTS 1, WALK 1**.

Augustus (63 BC-AD 14): The first Roman Emperor. Formerly called Octavian, he was the nephew and heir of Julius Caesar (see **A-Z**). After Caesar's assassination he shared power with Anthony and Lepidus, but following the defeat of Anthony and Cleopatra at Actium in 31 BC, he established himself as the leading figure in the state and was accepted as such by the Roman Senate, who conferred on him the title Augustus. He established peace and an effective government, inaugurated an ambitious building programme (including a new Forum - see **Fori Imperiali**), and, as patron of writers such as Horace, Virgil and Ovid, encouraged a flowering of literature. See **Ara Pacis Augustae**.

Baby-sitters: Ask at your hotel reception or *pensione*. If no baby-sitting service is available then try: *ARCI Donna Roma*, tel: 316449; *Centri di Solidarietà*, tel: 4280321; *La Ciliegia*, Via G. Soria 13, tel: 6275705.

Bernini, Gian Lorenzo (1598-1680): Painter, sculptor, architect, poet - considered the master of the Baroque style of architecture and sculpture. He designed the Baldacchino in St Peter's (see **CHURCHES 1**, **San Pietro in Vaticano**), the famous double colonnade surrounding the Piazza San Pietro (see **A-Z**), and many of the fountains and statuary that adorn the city. His technical virtuosity, energy and profound spiritual insight make his works among the most admired of his or any age.

Best Buys: The superb quality of Italian design is recognized worldwide, and shopping in Rome is a treat - if you can afford it! Leather goods, especially handbags and shoes, are recommended, and Rome is also an important centre for fashion, jewellery and antiques. But it must be emphasized, there are few bargains. See **SHOPPING**, **Shopping**.

Bicycle and Motorbike Hire: Cycling is not recommended in Rome, given the sheer volume of traffic and aggressive tactics of Roman drivers. Motorbikes and scooters are more practical, but should only be considered by those with experience and nerves of steel. *Collalti*, Via del Pellegrino 82, tel: 65441084; *Motonoleggio*, Via della Purificazione 66 (off Piazza Barberini), tel: 465485; *Scoot-a-Long*, Via Cavour 302, tel: 6780206.

Borgo: The medieval district on the right bank of the Tiber whose streets run north and south of the Via della Conciliazione. The Borgo (which means 'borough') was originally the site of Nero's Circus where St Peter suffered martyrdom. The area became popular with pilgrims visiting St Peter's (see **CHURCHES 1**, **San Pietro in Vaticano**), and the district was eventually fortified by the papacy in the 9thC. It was not formerly incorporated into the city of Rome until 1586. It is worth visiting for its ancient streets and houses, two Renaissance *palazzi* - the Palazzo Torlonia and the Palazzo Penitenzieri - and the church of Santo Spirito in Sassia, founded in 726 for Saxon pilgrims. See **CITY DISTRICTS**.

Borromini, Francesco Castelli (1599-1667): Architect, designer and artist. In contrast to his rival Bernini (see **A-Z**), his style is subtle and introverted. His architectural masterpiece and the epitome of High Baroque is the church of S Ivo alla Sapienza (1642-60) in the Palazzo della Sapienza, built for Urban VIII. He also collaborated with Bernini on the Palazzo Barberini (1625-33) which now houses the Galleria Nazionale d'Arte Antica (see **ART GALLERIES**, **A-Z**).

Bracciano: A delightful town, 40 km north west of Rome, set on a lush hillside above the circular Lago di Bracciano and dominated by the Castello Orsini-Odescalchi, a masterpiece of Renaissance military architecture. See **EXCURSION 4**.

Bramante, Donato (1444-1514): Architect and painter. He is most famous as the architect commissioned in 1505 by Julius II to rebuild St Peter's (see **CHURCHES 1**, **San Pietro in Vaticano**), although after his death his original Greek Cruciform design was considerably altered by later artists who continued the rebuilding, including Raphael (see **A-Z**), Sangallo and Michelangelo (see **A-Z**). He also created the *Tempietto* in the church of San Pietro in Montorio (see **CHURCHES 2**, **A-Z**) and the *Cortile del Belvedere* in the Vatican (see **A-Z**).

Budget:

Hotel Breakfast	L. 8000 - L. 12,000
Museum Ticket	L. 800 - L. 8000
Lunch	L. 15,000 - L. 100,000
Ice-cream	L. 1000 - L.10,000
Cinema Ticket	L. 5000
Dinner	L. 15,000 - L. 100,000+
Coffee	L. 800 - L.5000
Brandy	L. 4000

Buses: Buses are the main form of transport in Rome. The ATAC network covers the whole of the city. The main terminal and Information Office is in Piazza dei Cinquecento, outside Stazione Termini (see **Railways**), tel: 4695. The most popular bus is the No. 64 to St Peter's (see **CHURCHES 1**, **San Pietro in Vaticano**), which passes many tourist spots. Tickets should be bought in advance at booths at the bus terminal, or at tobacconists, bars and newspaper kiosks, and should be stamped in a machine on boarding. Single tickets are L. 700 (a book of ten is L. 6000); an integrated (B.I.G.) ticket for one day's unlimited travel on buses and the *Metropolitana* (see **Transport**) costs L. 2800. A weekly tourist ticket (L. 10,000) valid for the whole network can be obtained from the ATAC Information Office. Night buses, *Servizio Notturno*, run from midnight. Schedules are posted at bus stops, and you can buy a useful bus map of the city, detailing all services, from the terminus and from newsagents (L. 5000). See **Transport**.

Caesar, Julius (101-44 BC): Roman statesman and writer. At first he was subordinate to Pompey and Crassus, the leading figures in the state, but after a successful military campaign in Gaul (58-51 BC) he led his army to Rome (crossing the Rubicon) and challenged Pompey for

supremacy. He pursued Pompey to Egypt, where he installed Cleopatra on the throne and ultimately defeated his rival. After further successful campaigns in Africa and Spain he returned in triumph to Rome and was appointed Dictator (48 BC). He was responsible for the reconstruction of the Forum and the Basilica Giulia (see **WALK 1**, **Fori Imperiali**). He introduced political and institutional reforms, and devised measures to alleviate poverty and unemployment. However, his increasing personal power and ambition caused alarm among Republican opponents in the Senate, and he was assassinated on the Ides of March.

Cameras and Photography: Tripods and flashes are forbidden in museums. Film and photographic and video equipment are widely available but expensive: *Supermarket della Fotografia,* Via Tacinto 90a, tel: 3604857; *Fotottica Randazzo,* Piazza SS Apostoli 80, tel: 6787928; *Intercolor,* Via Marghera 33, tel: 492568. Fast processing service (one hour or less) is available at *Pronto Photo,* Via S Nicola da Tolentino 49, tel: 486424; *Fotouno,* Via Veneto 156, tel: 3610433.

Campidoglio: The most important of the seven hills of Rome and the political and religious centre of the ancient city. Its twin summits were the site of two important temples: Juno Moneta, and Jupiter Optimus Maximus Capitolinus, where newly elected senators were confirmed and victorious generals came to offer thanks to the gods. It is today the site of Michelangelo's Piazza del Campidoglio (see **SQUARES**, **WALK 4**, **A-Z**), on which stands the Palazzo Senatorio, the official residence of the Mayor of Rome.

Camping and Caravanning: The nearest camp sites to the city are on the main approach roads into Rome: *Roma,* Via Aurelia 831, tel: 6223018; *Flaminio,* Via Flaminia (8.2 km), tel: 3279006; *Nomentano,* Via della Cesarina 11, tel: 6100296; *Capitol,* Ostia Antica, Via Castelfusano 195, tel: 5662720.

Campo dei Fiori: See **Piazza Campo dei Fiori**.

Capitol: See **Campidoglio**.

Cappella Sistina

Cappella Sistina: Located in the Vatican Museums (see MUSEUMS 2, A-Z), the chapel was built between 1475 and 1480 by Baccio Pontelli for Pope Sixtus IV. The world-famous ceiling depicts scenes from the Book of Genesis and is one of Michelangelo's (see **A-Z**) masterpieces. The work was commissioned by Pope Julius II in 1508 and was finished four years later, an achievement of extraordinary artistic vision and physical endurance. Above the altar is *The Last Judgement,* with its violent and pessimistic imagery, begun by Michelangelo in 1533, only six years after the disastrous Sack of Rome. Later Popes found the nudity shocking and loincloths were painted over the figures. Overshadowed by these splendours, but of considerable interest, are the frescoes on the side walls depicting scenes from the life of Moses (on the right) and Christ (on the left), including Ghirlandaio's *The Calling of Peter and Andrew,* Perugino's *Christ Giving the Keys to St Peter,* Botticelli's *Moses Kills the Egyptian,* and others by Pinturicchio and Signorelli.

Caravaggio (1571-1610): The greatest Italian painter of the late 16th/early 17thC. He was notable for the eroticism of his earlier works, and, in his later religious output, for the realistic depiction of biblical characters, and the dramatic use of light and shadow used to enhance his figures. These characteristics are evident in his *Conversion of St Paul* and *Crucifixion of St Peter* in the Cerasi Chapel in S Maria del Popolo (see CHURCHES 1, **A-Z**). He fled Rome in 1606 after killing a man in a brawl, and spent the rest of his life wandering Naples and Sicily, constantly in trouble because of his violent temperament.

Car Hire: You need a valid driving licence which you have held for at least one year and you must also be over 21 years old. Unless you are paying by credit card you will have to leave a deposit. The main companies (Avis, Budget, Hertz, *etc*) have desks at Fiumicino and Ciampino (see **Airports**), and Stazione Termini (see **Railways**). See **Driving**.

Castel Gandolfo: A pretty town in the Castelli Romani on the lip of a crater above Lago Albano. It is famous as the Pope's summer residence. The palace (built in 1624 by Maderno) is set in superb gardens with an observatory at the back, but is not open to the public. Papal audiences are held each Wednesday from mid-July to early September. Tickets must be booked at the Vatican (see **A-Z**). The nearby church of San Tommaso da Villanova, built by Bernini (see **A-Z**) in 1661, offers beautiful views of the lake from its belvedere. See **EXCURSION 1**.

Castel Sant'Angelo: Begun by the Emperor Hadrian (see **A-Z**) towards the end of his reign for use as a family mausoleum, and completed by his successor, Antoninus Pius, in AD 139, one year after Hadrian's death. Because of its strategic position overlooking the Tiber, the mausoleum was used as a fortress from the 3rdC on, protecting the north-western approaches to the city. Its massive, reinforced walls made it a much appreciated sanctuary for successive popes, and a secret passage - *Passetto di Borgo* - was built to connect the castle to the Vatican (see **A-Z**). The castle took its name from a chapel dedicated to Sant'Angelo in Nubes, built to commemorate a heavenly vision of the Archangel Michael witnessed by Pope Gregory the Great in 590 when leading a procession to St Peter's (see **CHURCHES 1**, **San Pietro in**

Castel Sant'Angelo

Vaticano). In 1544, a statue of an angel, by Raffaello da Montelupo, was placed on top of the fortress. It was replaced by a bronze angel in 1753, but the marble original can still be seen inside the castle in the Court of the Angel. The mausoleum and fortress were subsequently used as a papal residence (visit the splendid papal chambers), a prison (where the Borgia popes incarcerated their enemies), and a military barracks (during the Napoleonic Occupation in the early 19thC). It was restored in the early 20thC and opened to the public as a museum (see MUSEUMS 1). Excellent views of the city can be enjoyed from the battlements and the loggias of Julius II and Paul III. See MONUMENTS 1, WALK 4.

Catacombe di Domitilla: The catacombs were used by Pagans and Christians as burial places, not, as is commonly thought, as refuges from persecution. This is probably the largest in Rome, and was established on land originally belonging to Domitilla, a Christian member of the Flavian imperial family. Near the entrance is the great basilica built on the tombs of Saints Nereus and Achilleus. From the basilica you enter an ancient plot where members of the Imperial family were interred; beyond are over 17 km of passages on four levels, containing many early Christian paintings and inscriptions. See MONUMENTS 3.

Catacombe di Priscilla: Named after Priscilla, a member of the patrician family gens Acilia and a victim of Diocletian's persecution. They contain frescoes of biblical scenes and 2ndC representations of the Virgin and Child, and the prophet Isaiah, some of the oldest such works in existence. See MONUMENTS 3.

Catacombe di San Calisto: A network of underground passages on four levels, estimated to contain 170,000 graves. Here you will find the famous Cappella dei Papi where numerous martyred 3rdC popes and bishops are buried. In an adjoining cubicle is the tomb of S Cecilia who suffered martyrdom in the 3rdC. Her remains are now in the church of S Cecilia in Trastevere (see CHURCHES 2, WALK 3). There is also an interesting 3rdC passage on which a series of cubicles open, called the Sacramental Chapels, containing frescoes of Baptism, Confession and the Last Supper. Other notable tombs include those of Pope

Eusebius (309-311) and Saints Calogeno and Partenio. Via Appia Antica 110. 0830-1200, 1430/1500-1900. Closed Wed. Buses 18, 218.

Catacombe di San Sebastiano: Here you can visit the 4thC basilica, the Chapel of Symbols containing early Christian inscriptions, and the crypt of Saint Sebastian, martyred during Diocletian's persecution. Via Appia Antica 136. 0830-1200, 1430-1800 Fri.-Wed. Bus 118.

Chemists: Chemists have the same opening times (see **A-Z**) as shops. Late night chemists: *Cristo Re Dei Ferr*, Termini; *De Luca*, Via Cavour 2; *Piram*, Via Nazionale 228. Dial 192 for addresses of chemists open outside normal hours, or check the notices displayed by all chemists.

Chiesa Nuova: More properly known as the church of S Maria in Vallicella, it was erected on the site of the former church of S Giovanni (12thC), hence *Chiesa Nuova*. It was started in 1575 by S Fillipo Neri, a leading figure of the Counter-Reformation, with the support of Pope Gregory XIII. The impressive facade is the work of Fausto Rughesi (1605) and inside are three altar paintings by Rubens and frescoes by Pietro da Cortona. Piazza della Chiesa Nuova.

Children: A large, busy city like Rome is not an ideal place for children, but there is a variety of attractions which should help keep them amused. Besides a trip to the Foro Romano or the Colosseo (see **MONUMENTS 1**, **WALK 1**, **A-Z**), which should excite the imagination, there are beautiful parks such as Villa Borghese (see **A-Z**), Villa Ada, and Villa Glori which have playgrounds, pony-riding, rollerskating, *etc.* Villa Borghese also contains a small zoo, the Giardino Zoologico (0830-sunset daily. M Flaminio. L. 5000). Luna Park in EUR (see **A-Z**) is the largest amusement park in Italy and offers plenty of thrills (Via delle Tre Fontane, EUR., 1600-2400 Mon.-Sat., 1000-2400 Sun. M EUR. Fermi). The Museo delle Cere is a wax museum displaying famous figures from Italian history (Piazza Santi Apostoli 67, 0900-2100 daily. Bus 64 to Piazza Venezia. L. 4000). The Piazza Navona (see **SQUARES**, **WALK 4**, **A-Z**), a traffic-free area with small street stalls selling toys and balloons, is also a popular spot with children. See **Baby-sitters**.

Cigarettes and Tobacco: Major international brands are available from *tabacchi* (which are designated by dark blue rectangular signs bearing a white T), bars and restaurants.

Cimitero Protestante: Round the corner from the Piramide di Caio Cestio (see **MONUMENTS 3**, **A-Z**) along the Via Caio Cestio is the entrance to the Protestant Cemetery. Here many artists are buried, including P. B. Shelley (1792-1822), E. Trelawny (1792-1881), Goethe's son Julius (d. 1830), and John Keats (1795-1821), whose tombstone bears the inscription 'Here lies one whose name was writ in water', added at the request of the poet on his deathbed. See **WALK 3**.

Circo Massimo: The grand stadium which, together with the Colosseo (see **MONUMENTS 1**, **WALK 1**, **A-Z**) provided entertainment for the population of ancient Rome. Chariot races and athletic contests held on its 1100 m racetrack drew crowds of up to 200,000 spectators. Today the Circus is a large grassy area amid the traffic. You can stroll along a raised strip which marks the top of the Spina - a wall that once separated the two halves of the racetrack. See **MONUMENTS 1**, **WALK 3**.

Climate: Spring is usually dry and sunny with temperatures ranging from 18°C to 28°C. Summers are hot and sometimes unbearably so, with temperatures soaring to 35°C-40°C at midday in July-Aug. Autumn is the best time to visit the city (October is perfect) - it is still warm, but not too hot for sightseeing, and less crowded. Winters are mild, and, although there is the odd frozen spell in January and February, snow is quite rare.

Colonna di Marco Aurelio: A marble column 29.6 m high and 3.7 m in diameter which dominates the Piazza Colonna (see **SQUARES**). Its shaft is ornamented with a relief rising in a spiral from the base to the enormous Doric capital surmounted by the bronze statue of St Paul erected in 1589. It was built between AD 180 and 196 to celebrate the victory of Marcus Aurelius over the Macromanni, Sarmatians and Quadi. Reliefs in the lower section represent the Germanic War (AD 171-173) and those in the upper, the Sarmatic War (AD 174-175); they provide a valuable insight into the military techniques and life of the period. Inside the column 190 stairs lead to the top. See **MONUMENTS 2**.

Colonna di Traiano: A marble column standing 38 m high, erected in AD 113 to commemorate the Emperor Trajan's wars with the Dacians (AD 101-102, 105-106). The 200 m spiral frieze has yielded a great deal of invaluable information about the weapons, uniforms and military tactics of the period. A golden statue of the Emperor which once surmounted the column was replaced in the Middle Ages by the figure of St Peter. See **WALK 1**, **Fori Imperiali**.

Colosseo: This massive but finely-proportioned structure was erected in the time of the Flavian Dynasty (AD 69-96, during the reigns of Vespasian, Titus and Domitian), and was originally known as the Amphitheatrum Flavium. It was given its present name after a colossal statue of Nero (see **A-Z**) which stood nearby. It could accommodate

Colosseo

50,000 spectators and was built on the site of a dried out lake-bed lined with sand and cement to bear the weight. Its inauguration in AD 80 initiated a long history of bloody and brutal animal fights, gladiator contests, athletic games and even mock naval battles, for which the centre of the arena could be flooded. See **MONUMENTS 1, WALK 1.**

Complaints: Ask to see the manager or owner of the premises if you find you have been overcharged or the price on the bill does not correspond to that displayed in the room. If you are still not satisfied contact the EPT (see **Tourist Information**) or the police (see **A-Z**); however, the threat of such action is usually sufficient.

Constantine (c. AD 277-337): Roman Emperor, known as Constantine the Great. In AD 312 he defeated his rival Maxentius at the Milvian Bridge in the north of Rome to become undisputed ruler of the Western Empire, and in subsequent campaigns defeated other rivals to consolidate his rule. He attributed his military success to divine intervention and was converted to Christianity. In AD 313 he issued the Edict of Milan, establishing freedom of worship for Christians, which signalled the inevitable demise of paganism. Several of the early Christian basilicas were begun during his reign, including the first Basilica di S Lorenzo fuori le Mura, S Giovanni in Laterano (see **CHURCHES 1**, **A-Z**) and the first church of St Peter's on the Vatican Hill. He also completed the secular Basilica of Maxentius in the Forum (see **Foro Romano**), and pieces of his colossal statue can be seen in the courtyard of the Palazzo dei Conservatori (see **Museo Capitolino**). For strategic reasons he moved the imperial capital to Constantinople in AD 330, and according to some sources, was baptized in AD 337 shortly before his death.

Consulates:
Australia - Via Alessandria 215. Tel: 841241.
Canada - Via G. B. de Rossi 27. Tel: 855341.
Republic of Ireland - Via del Pozzetto 105. Tel: 6782541.
New Zealand - Via Zara 28. Tel: 8541225.
United Kingdom - Via XX Settembre 80/a. Tel: 4755441.
USA - Via Vittorio Veneto 119/a. Tel: 4674.

Conversion Charts:

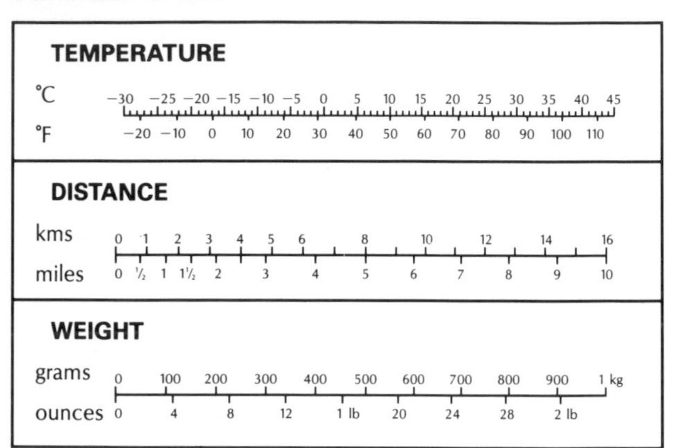

Crime and Theft: Keep all valuables and large amounts of cash in the hotel safe. Carry your wallet in a secure pocket and keep handbags under the arm as opposed to over the shoulder. Never leave baggage unattended or visible in a locked car. Keep the serial numbers of your traveller's cheques separately, along with a note of your passport number; if they are lost or stolen notify the office where they were issued immediately. If you lose your passport then notify the police (see **Emergencies**, **A-Z**) and your consulate (see **A-Z**). Carry car documents with you to prove ownership in case of theft. Keep a copy of police reports for insurance claims (see **A-Z**).

Currency: The Italian monetary unit is the lira (plural lire), often written L. before the figure. Coins in circulation are 10, 20, 50, 100, 200 and 500 lire; notes are in denominations of 1000, 2000, 5000, 10,000, 50,000 and 100,000 lire. L. 10 and L. 20 coins are scarce and small change is often given in the form of *gettoni* (telephone tokens - see **Money**, **Telephones and Telegrams**).

Customs:

Duty Paid Into:	Cigarettes (or)	Cigars (or)	Tobacco	Spirits	Wine
E.E.C.	300	75	400 g	1.5 *l*	5 *l*
U.K.	300	75	400 g	1.5 *l*	5 *l*

Disabled: There are toilets for the disabled at Fiumicino and Ciampino (see **Airports**), at Stazione Termini (see **Railways**), near platform 1, and at Piazza S Pietro (see **SQUARES**, **A-Z**). Most buildings and the old streets are ill-equipped for wheelchairs. Mention any special needs when making hotel or restaurant reservations. For more details, contact the EPT (see **Tourist Information**).

Drinks: Ask for the house wine (*il vino della casa*) in cheaper restaurants, as this is usually good value. Most establishments offer a varied selection of wines, including local favourites such as Frascati and Marino, and national varieties such as Chianti and Orvieto. Carbonated mineral water (*acqua minerale*) is very popular, and there is usually a selection of beers (*birra*) and fruit juices. Coffee (*un caffè*) is espresso, small and strong; for coffee with a drop of milk order a *caffellatte*; cappuccino is made with frothy milk sprinkled with chocolate. Tea is also widely available, with milk or lemon (*al limone*). *Grappa* is a strong grape-skin liqueur made in the north of Italy, and is popular after meals.

Driving: Driving in Rome can be a nerve-wracking and frustrating experience due to severe congestion, a confusing one-way system, the closure of many central streets to traffic, and severe competition for the limited parking spaces available. If you do venture onto the roads then remember to drive on the right, and give way to traffic coming from the right - although these rules are not always followed! The speed limit in built-up areas is nominally 50 kph; on motorways 130 kph Mon.-Fri., 110 kph Sat. & Sun. Third Party insurance is obligatory if bringing your own car, and make sure you have your driving licence, car registration papers and a national identity sticker. You must also carry a red warning triangle in case of breakdowns (see **Accidents and Breakdowns**). Petrol coupons (giving discounts for petrol) and motorway vouchers (for use at motorway tolls) are available for foreign motorists bringing their own cars (not if you hire a car). These are available from automobile associations at home or Automobile Club Italiano (ACI) branches at border crossings (not within Italy). See **Parking**, **Petrol**.

Drugs: All drugs are illegal and there are severe penalties for offenders. Contact your embassy or consulate (see **A-Z**) if you are arrested for a drugs-related offence.

Electricity: 220V. Two-pin plugs are used and adaptors are widely available in Italy and the UK.

E.U.R.

E.U.R.

Emergencies:

Emergency (Police/Fire/Ambulance)	113
Ambulance and Red Cross	5100
Carabinieri	212121
City Police	67691
Fire Brigade	44441
ACI Breakdown Service	116

See **Crime and Theft**, **Health**, **Police**.

EUR (Esposizione Universale Romana): This modern suburban complex, 5 km south of the city, was begun by Mussolini in 1938, and intended as a showpiece of Fascist urban design to be revealed at Rome's World Fair in 1942. However, the Second World War intervened and work did not resume until 1952. The huge Palazzo dello Sport (Via Cristoforo Colombo), designed by Pier Luigi Nervi for the 1960 Olympics, is perhaps the best example of modern architecture in Rome. Of particular interest are the following:
Museo della Civiltà Romana (Museum of Roman Civilization), Piazzale Giovanni Agnelli 10. This museum was a gift from the FIAT company to the city of Rome. It features plaster casts of ancient monuments, including the Colonna di Traiano (see **A-Z**). 0900-1400, 1700-2000 Tues. & Thurs., 0900-1400 Wed. & Fri., 0900-1300 Sun.
Museo delle Arti e delle Tradizioni Popolari, Piazza Marconi 8. Houses a large collection of exhibits illustrating daily life in Rome at the end of the last century. 0900-1400 Tues.-Sat., 0900-1300 Sun.
M EUR Fermi or EUR Marconi. Bus 93 from Stazione Termini (see **Railways**) or 97 from Piazza Sonnino. By car, follow Via Cristoforo Colombo from Piazza Ardeatina.

Events: *January*: *Befana*, the toys and sweets fair on the Piazza Navona (see **A-Z**), ends 6 Jan. *February*: Carnival and Lenten celebrations - young children dress up and shower the streets with water and flour bombs. *March*: Feast of St Joseph celebrated in the Trionfale district, where traditional hot fritters are served from stalls in the streets (19th). *April*: Holy Week. Religious services celebrated in all Rome's churches. *Good Friday*: The Pope takes part in the Stations of the Cross:

Fontana di Trevi

the procession begins at the Colosseo (see **MONUMENTS 1**, **A-Z**) and ends on the Palatino (see **A-Z**); *Easter Day*: At noon the Pope gives the blessing *Urbi et Orbi* from the loggia of St Peter's (see **CHURCHES 1**, **San Pietro in Vaticano**); Celebration of the founding of Rome, in Piazza del Campidoglio - see **SQUARES**, **A-Z** (21st); Azalea Show in the Piazza di Spagna (see **SQUARES**, **A-Z**): the most beautiful azalea blooms from the city's nurseries are displayed on the Spanish Steps (second half of April). *May*: Antique Fair in Via dei Coronari (mid-May); Art exhibition in Via Margutta (8th-11th); Rose Show in Valle Murcia rosery on the Aventino (1 May-15 June). *June*: Feast of St John the Baptist - various events take place in the San Giovanni district - traditionally, large quantities of snails are consumed (24th) ; International Trade Fair (Fiera di Roma), Via Cristoforo Colombo (until 15th). *July*: Feast of Noiantri - the people of Trastevere (see **CITY DISTRICTS**, **WALK 3**, **A-Z**) hold folk concerts and sports contests in honour of their ancestors; Estate Musica and Estate Romana - cultural entertainments organized by the Rome EPT (see **Tourist Information**) and municipality (June-Sept.). *August*: Festa delle Catene, in the church of San Pietro in Vincoli - see **CHURCHES 3**, **WALK 2**, **A-Z** (1st); Festa della Madonna della Neve, in Santa Maria Maggiore (see **CHURCHES 1**, **WALK 2**, **A-Z**). *September*: Children's Expo at the Fiera di Roma; National Antique Fair at the Fiera di Roma. *October*: Art Fair in Via Margutta; Handicraft Trade Fair, in Via dell'Orso. *November*: Rome Motor Show, at the Fiera di Roma. *December*: Festa della Madonna Immacolata, in Piazza di Spagna; Toy and Sweet Fair, at Piazza Navona (Dec 15-Jan 6); Solemn Te Deum, in the church of Il Gesù - see **CHURCHES 1**, **Gesù** (31st); beautiful Nativity scenes are displayed in many churches throughout the city.

Fontana di Trevi: The largest and most famous fountain in Rome, designed by Nicola Salvi for Pope Clement XII and completed in 1762. Built into the rear of the Palazzo Poli, it is fed by the waters of the 'Acqua Vergine' (built by Agrippa in the 1stC BC), and depicts the figure of Oceanus (Neptune) with sea-horses, tritons and shells. It is traditional for visitors to throw coins into the large basin to ensure their return to the city.

Food: Roman meals usually start with *antipasti*, and you are often able to serve yourself from a delicious selection of cooked and raw vegetables, seafood, omelettes and salads. Traditionally this is followed by a pasta course. Typical Roman offerings are: *Spaghetti alla carbonara* (bacon, garlic, and beaten egg); *Penne all'arrabbiata* (pasta tubes with a spicy tomato sauce); *Spaghetti all'amatriciana* (tomato sauce with salt pork, or ham); and *Gnocchi* (potato dumplings in a sauce). Popular main courses include: *Saltimbocca* (veal fillet with ham and sage cooked in white wine); *Ossobuco* (stewed veal knuckles); *Abbacchio* (roast lamb); *Pollo alla cacciatore* (chicken with tomato and herb sauce); and *Trippa* (tripe). The meal is usually completed with cheeses such as *Pecorino* (made from ewe's milk) or fresh *Mozzarella*, fruit, or *gelato* (ice-cream), an Italian speciality which comes in many exotic flavours. See **RESTAURANTS**, **Drinks**, **Restaurants**.

Fori Imperiali: The Fori Imperiali include the Forums of the Emperors Julius Caesar (see **A-Z**), Augustus (see **A-Z**), Trajan, Nerva and Vespasian, and are situated to the north west of the earlier Foro Romano (see **A-Z**). Most of the ruins are concealed by modern buildings, and by the broad swathe of Mussolini's Via dei Fori Imperiali. Of the Foro di Cesare (54-46 BC), at the foot of the Campidoglio (see **A-Z**), little remains apart from three columns of the Temple of Venus Genetrix which once housed Julius Caesar's collection of sculptures and Greek paintings. All that remains of the Foro di Augusto are three massive Corinthian columns belonging to the Temple of Mars Ultor (Mars the Avenger) built in 2 BC. Nearby is the Casa dei Cavalieri di Rodi (House of the Knights of Rhodes), which offers unrivalled views over the five forums. Apart from two Corinthian columns from the Temple of Minerva, the Foro di Nerva is almost entirely obscured by the Via dei Fori Imperiali, as is the Foro di Vespasiano, whose major building was incorporated into the church of S Cosma e Damiano (see **CHURCHES 3, WALK 1**). The Foro di Traiano, designed by Apollodorus of Damascus in AD 107 and completed in AD 143, included a triumphal arch, Greek and Latin libraries, the Basilica Ulpia, and a sumptuous temple, although practically nothing of these structures survives with the exception of the magnificent Colonna di Traiano (see **A-Z**). To the north are the remains of the Mercati di Traianei (Trajan's Markets) a semicircular three-tiered complex, once a thriving shopping and commercial centre. See **MONUMENTS 2, WALK 1**.

Foro Romano: Originally a marshy area between the hills of Campidoglio (see **WALK 4**, **A-Z**) and Palatino (see **WALK 1**, **A-Z**), the land was drained and gradually developed over a period of 1000 years into the centre of religious, political and commercial life in ancient Rome. From the 8thC on the area fell into disuse, the ruined structures were incorporated into churches and fortresses, or used as quarries, and the area became the *Campo Vaccino*, used for cattle pasture, until serious excavations began in the 18th and 19thCs. Today, the jumble of ruins remains surprisingly evocative of the power and glory of the ancient city. Among the more interesting ruins are: the Arco di Tito (Arch of Titus), standing at the eastern end of the site, the oldest surviving tri-

umphal arch (AD 81), with reliefs depicting Titus' suppression of the Jewish revolt; the Tempio di Vesta (Temple of Vesta) where the Vestal Virgins tended the sacred flame (see **MONUMENTS 3**, **WALK 3**, **A-Z**) and the Atrium di Vesta (House of the Vestals); the Tempio di Antonio e Faustina (Temple of Antonius Pius and Faustina), consecrated by the Senate in AD 141; the Tempio di Castore e Polluce (Temple of Castor and Pollux) first built in 484 BC and restored by the Emperor Tiberius during the 1stC AD; the Tempio di Saturno (Temple of Saturn), many times rebuilt, but originally dating from c. 497 BC, and the one most venerated by the Romans; the Arco di Settimio Severo (Arch of Septimius Severus) erected in AD 203 in honour of the victories of Septimius Severus and his sons over the Parthians - this was the prototype for the Arco di Constantino (see **MONUMENTS 1**, **A-Z**); and the Colonna di Phocas (Column of Phocas), a 14 m high Corinthian column dedicated to the Byzantine Emperor, erected in AD 608, the last monument added in ancient times. See **MONUMENTS 1**, **WALK 1**.

Galleria Barberini: The Galleria Nazionale d'Arte Antica is housed in the Palazzo Barberini, an imposing Baroque palace to the east of the Quirinale, begun by Maderno and Borromini (see **A-Z**) in 1625 and completed with the aid of Bernini (see **A-Z**) in 1633. The main feature of the palazzo is the *Salone* (Great Hall), which has a ceiling fresco by Pietro da Cortona (*Triumph of Divine Providence*). Amongst the greatest treasures contained in the collection are: *La Fornarina* by Raphael (see **A-Z**), a portrait of the artist's mistress (who was a baker's daughter); Holbein's *Henry VIII*; Filippino Lippi's delightful *Madonna*; two magnificent El Greco's, *The Adoration of the Shepherds* and *Nativity and Baptism of Christ*; Titian's *Venus and Adonis*; and Tintoretto's *Christ and Mary Magdalene*. See **ART GALLERIES**.

Galleria Borghese: The Casino Borghese was completed in 1615 for Cardinal Scipione Borghese, nephew of Pope Paul V and a great patron of Bernini (see **A-Z**). It is situated in the eastern part of the Villa Borghese (see **A-Z**), off Via Pinciana. The works of art collected within the Casino are of the highest quality. The ground floor is devoted mainly to sculpture, the first floor to paintings. Among the attractions are: Canova's alluring sculpture of *Pauline Borghese,* sister of Napoleon, one of his most original works (Room I); Bernini's famous *David,* commissioned by Cardinal Borghese - the features are said to be those of the artist, and legend has it that Borghese himself held the mirror for Bernini while he worked (Room II); in Room III, Bernini's *Apollo and Daphne,* which brilliantly captures Daphne's metamorphosis into a laurel bush while being chased by Apollo; *The Rape of Proserpine,* again by Bernini, can be found in Room IV, and *Aeneas, Anchises and Ascanius Fleeing from the Sack of Troy,* in which the sculptor collaborated with his father Pietro, is in Room VI.
Upstairs, it is difficult to be selective about the paintings as most of them are genuine masterpieces. They include: *The Deposition* by Raphael (see **A-Z**) and Pinturicchio's fine *Crucifixion of Saints Jerome and Christopher* in Room IX; a *Madonna with Child* by Andrea del Sarto in Room X; Domenichino's *Sibyl,* also known as *Music,* in Room XII and his *Diana with her Nymphs* in Room XIV; also in Room XIV, the unforgettable *Boy with a Basket of Fruit* and *David and Goliath* by Caravaggio (see **A-Z**); and Titian's masterpiece, *Sacred and Profane Love,* in Room XX. See **ART GALLERIES.**

Galleria Doria-Pamphili: The Pamphili and Doria families' art collection is exhibited here in the Palazzo Doria where they still live. Among the art treasures are: Titian's *Spain Succouring Religion,* and *Salome*; three brilliant paintings by Caravaggio (see **A-Z**) - *St Mary Magdalen, St John the Baptist,* and *The Rest on the Flight into Egypt*; Alessandro Algardi's bust of *Olimpia Maidalchini,* the sister-in-law of Pope Innocent X, whose own portrait by Velázquez can be seen further along the hall; several exquisite 17thC French landscapes by Claude Lorrain; and the *Flight into Egypt* by Annibale Carracci (c. 1604).
See **ART GALLERIES.**

Galleria Nazionale d'Arte Antica: See **Galleria Barberini**.

Galleria Nazionale d'Arte Moderna: Important collection of 19th and 20thC Italian sculpture and painting, including works by the Italian Impressionists (*Macchiaioli*), Futurists such as Umberto Boccioni, and Metaphysical artists like Giorgio de Chirico. See **ART GALLERIES**.

Gesù: Built between 1568 and 1584 as the 'flagship' of the Counter Reformation, this church became a model for Jesuit churches all over Europe. The facade was designed by Giacomo della Porta, and the incredibly rich interior decoration is by Vignola. See the magnificent fresco of the *Triumph of the Name of Jesus* by Giovanni Battista Gaulli on the ceiling of the nave, and the opulent *Tomb of St Ignatius Loyola* by Andrea Pozzo, which is topped by the largest known piece of lapis lazuli. Gilded sculptures, coloured marble and skilful *trompe l'oeil* paintings make the Gesù the prototype of the early Baroque style. See **CHURCHES 1**.

Hadrian (AD 76-138): Emperor (117-138), notable as a great builder, traveller and lover of art and philosophy. In Rome he was responsible for the Castel Sant'Angelo (see **MONUMENTS 1**, **MUSEUMS 1**, **WALK 4**, **A-Z**), and the Pantheon (see **MONUMENTS 1**, **WALK 4**, **A-Z**). He also built great frontier fortifications - the famous wall in Britain and the Limes in Germany. During his travels he visited practically every province of the Empire, and was especially fond of Athens and the culture of Classical Greece, as is evident in his final great project, the magnificent Villa Adriana near Tivoli (see **EXCURSION 3**, **Tivoli**).

Hairdressers: These are distributed widely throughout the city and some of the more luxurious hotels have their own salons. *Intercoiffure*, Corso del Rinascimento 6 (Piazza Navona), tel: 6543698; *Giannie Michele*, Via G. Carducci 16 (for men), tel: 4818722.

Health: Before leaving the UK you should obtain form E 111 from the Department of Social Security, which entitles you to free medical treatment while you are in Italy. Present the form to any (State) doctor you consult, who will then arrange for you to be exempted from payment. You should also take out a private insurance policy to cover the costs of repatriation in case of serious illness (see **Insurance**).
The principal hospitals are:
Policlinico Umberto I, Viale del Policlinico, tel: 4997.
San Camillo Hospital, Circonvallazione Gianicolense 87, tel: 58701
San Giovanni Hospital, Via Ambra Aradam 8, tel: 77051.
Santo Spirito Hospital, Lungotevere in Sassia 1, tel: 650901.
G. Eastman Dental Hospital, Viale Regina Elena 287, tel: 491949.
For urgent blood transfusions, tel: 7575893.
See **Chemists**, **Emergencies**.

Insurance: You should take out travel insurance to cover you against theft and loss of property and money, as well as medical expenses, for the duration of your stay. Your travel agent should be able to recommend a suitable policy. See **Crime and Theft**, **Driving**, **Health**.

Ponte Fibrisio, Isola Tiberino

Isola Tiberina: The island is linked to Trastevere (see CITY DISTRICTS, **A-Z**) on the right bank by Ponte Sestio, and to the Cenci district on the left bank by the ancient Ponte Fabricio (built in 62 BC). It was the site of the Temple of Aesculapius (the god of medicine), after a serpent, which had been brought to Rome from Epidaurus in Greece, supposedly cured the great plague of 291 BC, and subsequently chose the island as its home. Amongst the notable sights here are the medieval Torre dei Caetani, and the beautiful church of San Bartolomeo on its peaceful *piazza*. See MONUMENTS 3, WALK 3.

Keats-Shelley Memorial House: The house where the English poet John Keats (1795-1821) resided for a time in the early 19thC with his companion Joseph Severn is now a library and museum containing memorabilia of Keats and his fellow poet Percy Bysshe Shelley (1792-1822), who both died in Italy and are buried in the Cimitero Protestante (see **A-Z**). You can visit Keats's bedroom and see his death mask. See MUSEUMS 1.

Largo di Torre Argentina: Named after the nearby Torre Argentina, a 16thC house built into an existing tower. The ruins of several Republican Temples were discovered here in the 1920s below street level, and can be viewed from the railings above. The Teatro Argentina on the west side of the square was the venue for the first performance, in 1816, of Rossini's *Barber of Seville*, which was booed by the audience.

Laundries: Ask at your hotel or *pensione*. Laundrettes in Rome are not self-service: you leave your washing and will be told when to collect it. The price depends on the weight of clothes. In the city centre try: *Scerna*, Largo Magnagrecia 22; *Zampa*, Piazza Campo dei Fiori 38.

Lost Property: Report any loss or theft to the police immediately. There are Lost Property Offices at all airports (see **A-Z**) and railway termini (see **A-Z**). *Municipal Transport (ATAC)* Via Volturno 65, near Stazione Termini, 0900-1200; *Municipal Lost Property Office*, Via Niccolò Bettoni 1, 0900-1200. See **Police**.

Mausoleo di Augusto: A large cylindrical marble tomb with a conical earthen mound on top which reaches to a height of 44 m and is surrounded by cypress trees. It was built by the Emperor Augustus (see **A-Z**) for himself and members of the Julio-Claudian family. It fell into disrepair and was used in the 12thC as a fortress by the Colonna family, as a quarry for its travertine stone, and in the later 19thC as a concert hall and circus. Piazza Augusto Imperatore. Bus 90, 95. See **WALK 2.**

Metropolitana: See **Transport**.

Michelangelo (1474-1564): Most famous as the painter of the Sistine Chapel (see **Cappella Sistina**), although he was also an architect, draughtsman and poet. He spent his life in Florence and Rome working alternately under the patronage of the Medicis and Pope Julius II. In Rome he created the famous *Pietà* in St Peter's (see **CHURCHES 1**, **San Pietro in Vaticano**) in1499, and then embarked on two massive projects for Julius II - the Sistine Ceiling (1508-12), and the 40 figures intended for Julius' tomb, the most famous of which is *Moses* (1513-16), now in S Pietro in Vincoli (see **CHURCHES 3**, **A-Z**). He worked in Florence 1516-34, then returned to Rome and worked on the *Last Judgement* in the Sistine (1536-41). His architectural achievements include the Piazza del Campidoglio (see **SQUARES**, **A-Z**) and the dome of St Peter's.

Pietà

Money: Foreign currency and traveller's cheques can be changed in banks, bureaux de change (*cambio*) and larger hotels on the production of a passport. Major credit cards are widely accepted and many shops and hotels also accept payment by traveller's cheques or in foreign currency, but often charge a high commission (check the rate they offer first). There are exchange bureaux at: Stazione Termini (see **Railways**); Piazza di Spagna 38 (American Express); *Aurum*, Via delle Vite 18;

Cambio Roma, Via G. Crispi 15; *Società Rosati,* Via Nazionale 186; *Via Viaggi,* Via Due Macelli 109; *Eurocambio,* Via F. Crispi 92.
See **Currency**.

Monumento a Vittorio Emanuele II: Built between 1885 and 1911, this conspicuous marble monument (135 m long and 70 m high) overlooks the Piazza Venezia (see **SQUARES**) and commemorates the first king of a united Italy (d. 1878). On the lower terrace is the Tomb of the Unknown Soldier and the Altare della Patria (Altar of the Fatherland). The upper terrace commands superb views over the city. Piazza Venezia. See **SQUARES, WALK 1, WALK 4**.

Mura Aureliane: A wall measuring 19 km in circumference which surrounds the ancient city. It was built between AD 272 and 279 by the Emperor Aurelian to protect Rome from the Alemanni, whom he had defeated a few years previously. Today the wall encloses one tenth of the population of the city. It is best seen between Porta San Paolo (see **WALK 3, A-Z**) and Porta Latina in the south, and at Porta Pinciana to the north west. See **MONUMENTS 3**.

Museo Baracco: A small collection of Roman, Greek, Assyrian, Egyptian and Etruscan sculpture presented to the city by Baron Giovanni Baracco in 1902. The collection is housed in the Palazzo Piccola Farnesina, designed by Antonio da Sangallo the Younger in 1523 for the French Cardinal Thomas Le Roy. 0900-1400 Tues.-Sat., 0900-1300 Sun., also 1700-2000 Tues. & Thurs. L. 2000. Corso Vittorio Emanuele II 68. Bus 64 from Stazione Termini. See **WALK 4**.

Museo Capitolino: An important collection of sculpture and painting housed in two *palazzi* on either side of Michelangelo's (see **A-Z**) Piazza del Campidoglio (see **SQUARES, WALK 4, A-Z**).
The Palazzo Nuovo, on the left, has mostly classical statuary, notably the *Capitoline Venus,* a Roman copy of a beautiful Greek original, the poignant *Dying Gaul,* and the *Marble Faun.* There is also the Room of the Emperors, featuring 65 busts of Roman emperors, politicians and philosophers. In the courtyard fountain is the statue of *Marforio,* a river

god. Across the square, in the Palazzo dei Conservatori, you can find the symbol of Rome, the *Capitoline She-Wolf*, in the Sala della Lupa. The wolf is a 6thC BC Etruscan bronze; Romulus and Remus are 15thC additions. See too the *Spinario*, the boy plucking a thorn from his foot. The Pinacoteca Capitolina (in the same building) houses a number of masterpieces by Titian, Caravaggio (see **A-Z**) - including the superb *St John the Baptist*, Guercino (*Burial and Reception into Heaven of St Petronilla*), Rubens and Van Dyck. The stone head, hand and foot lying in the courtyard are all that is left of a colossal statue of Emperor Constantine (see **A-Z**). The museums are spectacularly floodlit on Saturday nights from 2030-2300. See MUSEUMS 1.

Museo Nazionale Romano: A large and important collection of Roman antiquities housed in part of the Terme di Diocleziano (see MONUMENTS 2, **A-Z**), adjacent to the church of S Maria degli Angeli. Only the best pieces are on display, and countless others are hidden away in storerooms. Among the treasures are the magnificent *Ludovisi Throne* (5thC BC), decorated with a relief depicting the birth of Aphrodite; the *Daughter of Niobe* (Greek 5thC BC), *The Discus Thrower*, a copy of the statue by Myron; and the *Girl of Anzio* (Greek 4thC BC) unearthed at Anzio in 1878. On the first floor, don't miss the collection of frescoes and mosaics, especially the examples recovered from the Casa di Livia on the Palatino (see WALK 1, **A-Z**). See MUSEUMS 1.

Music: Opera and ballet are performed (December-June) at the Teatro dell'Opera (Piazza Beniamino Gigli 1). Tickets are available 48 hours before the performance begins (Box Office open 1000-1300, 1700-1900 Tues.-Sat.). During the summer (July-August) the theatre moves to the Terme di Caracalla (see **A-Z**) - tickets on sale on the day of the performance. Orchestral concerts by the famous Accademia di Santa Cecilia are held in the Auditorio di Via della Conciliazione (Via della Conciliazione 4), and the Accademia Filarmonica performs in the Teatro Olimpico (Piazza Gentile da Fabriano 17). Various basilicas hold one-off performances of recitals and choral concerts, and there are music festivals in the parks during the summer. There are also live music venues including jazz and rock clubs (see NIGHTLIFE, **Nightlife**).

Nero (AD 37-68): Convinced of his artistic genius and preoccupied with composing music and poetry rather than governing, his rule (58-68) degenerated into a reign of terror and debauchery – he murdered both his wife and mother. He is thought to have been responsible for the great fire of AD 64, for which he blamed the Christians and made them suffer cruelly. Outlawed by the Senate for military and political failures, he committed suicide. His Domus Aurea (see WALK 2) was one of the most sumptuous of imperial residences and the Colosseo (see MONUMENTS 1, WALK 1, **A-Z**) was named after the colossal statue of him which once stood near the site of the Circo Massimo (see **A-Z**).

Newspapers: Foreign newspapers and magazines are widely available in kiosks and newsagents all over the city.

Nightlife: There is a variety of bars, nightclubs, discos and music venues to suit all tastes. Theatres usually present productions of de Filippo, Goldoni, Pirandello and other classics, *eg* Eliseo (Via Nazionale 183), Parioli (Via Borsi 20) and Argentina (Largo Torre Argentina). The Sistina (Via Sistina 129-130) features musicals and international variety acts. Box offices usually open 1000-1300, 1600-1900, but times do vary. For movie-goers, the Pasquino (Vicolo del Piede 19a, off Piazza S Maria in Trastevere) is one of the few cinemas which show English-language films in the original (usually two/three showings starting at 1600. Cost L. 5000). See NIGHTLIFE, **Music**.

Opening Times: These can vary enormously, but generally:
Banks - 0830-1330, 1500-1600 Mon.-Fri.
Retail shops - 0900-1300, 1600-1930 (closed Mon. a.m. & Sun.);
Supermarkets and food shops - 0800-1330, 1700-1930 (closed Sat. p.m. in summer, Thurs. p.m. in winter).
Churches - 0700-1200, 1600-1900.
Museums - 0900/1000-1300/1400, 1400/1500-1700/1800 (1300 Sun. & hols.) Tues.-Sun. Note that ticket offices usually close half-an-hour to one hour before museums close.
Post Offices - 0800-1400 Mon.-Sat.
See **Public Holidays**, **What's On**.

Ostia Antica: The important and exciting remains of the ancient port of Rome, which was founded c. 300 BC. The excavations have revealed a great deal of invaluable evidence concerning day-to-day life in ancient Rome and are well worth a day-trip from the city. 23 km west of Rome. Train/Metro services from Stazione Termini (see **Railways**). See **EXCURSION 2**.

Palatino: According to legend, it was on this hill that Romulus first marked out the limits of the city with his plough in 753 BC. It was chosen by the subsequent rulers of the Republic and the Empire as the site of their sumptuous palaces, lavishly decorated with frescoes and marble sculptures. See **WALK 1**.

Palazzo Barberini: See **Galleria Barberini**.

Palazzo Borghese: This palace was designed by Vignola in 1560 and completed by Ponzio in 1614 as the summer residence of Cardinal Camillo Borghese, who later became Pope Paul V (1605-21). Known as *Il Cembalo* (The Harpsichord) because of its unusual shape, it housed the family's magnificent art collection until it was transferred to the Casino of the Villa Borghese in 1891 (see **Galleria Borghese**). Piazza Borghese. M Spagna.

Palazzo Doria: See **Galleria Doria-Pamphili**.

Palazzo Farnese: The most impressive Renaissance palace in the city. It was begun by Antonio da Sangallo the Younger in 1514 and taken over by Michelangelo in 1546. The first floor is decorated with superb frescoes by Annibale Caracci. It has been the home of the French Embassy since 1871, and is not open to the public. Piazza Farnese. See **WALK 4**.

Palazzo Piccola Farnesina: See **Museo Baracco**.

Palazzo del Quirinale: This palace was begun in 1574 by Flaminio Ponzio and extended in stages by Fontana, Maderno, Bernini (see **A-Z**) and Fuga. From 1592, when Clement VIII moved here from the Vatican (see **A-Z**), the Quirinale became the favourite summer residence of the popes. Since 1947 it has been the official residence of the Italian President. For permission to visit, apply to the Ufficio Intendenza, Palazzo Quirinale, Roma 00137. Piazza del Quirinale. M Barberini.

Palazzo Spada: Originally dating from 1540, the palace was restored by Borromini (see **A-Z**) in 1632 - his *trompe l'oeil* colonnade which links two interior courtyards is its most interesting feature. It has been the seat of the Italian Council of State since 1889 and also houses the Galleria Spada (see **ART GALLERIES**), a small collection of 17th and 18thC paintings assembled by Cardinal Bernardino Spada (1594-1661) and his family. See **WALK 4**.

Palazzo Venezia: One of the earliest palaces to be built in Rome, it was begun in c. 1455 (architect unknown) for Cardinal Pietro Barbo, afterwards Pope Paul II (1464-71). From 1564-1797 it was the property of the Republic of Venice, while Mussolini later used it as his official residence, and delivered many of his speeches from the balcony overlooking the Piazza. The Museo di Palazzo Venezia (see **MUSEUMS 1**) contains medieval and Renaissance paintings, sculpture, tapestries, ceramics and silver. See **WALK 4**.

Pantheon: One of the best preserved and most impressive examples of ancient Roman architecture. It was built by the Emperor Hadrian (see **A-Z**) in AD 120-125 on the site of an earlier monument erected in 27 BC by Consul Marcus Agrippa. The emperor was modest enough to retain the original inscription, 'M. AGRIPPA L. F. COS TERTIUM FECIT' (Marcus Agrippa, son of Lucius, Consul for the third time, built this). The impressive portico with its 16 granite columns leads you to the huge bronze doors and into the interior of the monument. Its many treasures, mostly bronze and marble sculpture, have been plundered long since, but the building itself, and the amazing dome, remain much as they were nearly 2000 years ago. The dome, 43 m across, is larger than that of St Peter's (see **CHURCHES 1**, **San Pietro in Vaticano**), and the sunlight streaming through the oculus (the opening at the dome's apex)

Pantheon

lends a unique atmosphere to the interior. The monument was Christianized by Pope Boniface IV in 608, and dedicated to the martyrs whose bones were brought from the catacombs and reburied here. The Italian kings Vittorio Emanuele II and Umberto I, and the artist Raphael (see **A-Z**) are also interred here. See MONUMENTS 1, WALK 4.

Parking: Parking in Rome is a nightmare. Cars far outnumber parking places, and double and triple parking is normal. There are official car parks on all the main routes into the city centre, and the largest city car park is under the Villa Borghese (see **A-Z**). Illegally-parked cars are towed away by the Traffic Police. Should this happen, contact the Commando dei Vigili Urbani, Via della Conciliazione 4 (tel: 676938).

Passports and Customs: A valid passport (or identity card for some EC visitors) is necessary, but no visa is required for stays of less than three months. There is no limit on the amount of money you can bring in or out of the country, but amounts over a million lire must be declared on the V 2 form you fill out on entry.

Petrol: There are petrol stations situated at frequent intervals along all the major routes into and out of the city (open 0700-1230, 1500-1900 Oct.-Apr.; 0700-1230, 1530-1930 May-Sept.). Central petrol stations with extended opening hours: Appio Tuscolano - *Total*, Via Appia/Via Cessati Spiriti; Flaminio - *Mobil*, Corso Francia/Via di Vigna Stelluti; Trastevere - *Agip*, Lungotevere Ripa 8.

Pets: Domestic pets must have a veterinary certificate stating that the animal is in good health, and has been vaccinated against rabies between 20 days and 11 months prior to entering Italy. In public, dogs must be either muzzled or kept on a leash at all times.

Piazza Bocca della Verità: Built on the site of the Forum Boarium, an ancient cattle market. From here there are views over an eclectic mix of buildings including: the Romanesque church of S Maria in Cosmedin (see CHURCHES 2, **A-Z**), the portico of which contains the famous Bocca della Verità (Mouth of Truth), an oracle used in trials by

Piazza Campo dei Fiori

ordeal - the suspect's hand was placed inside and, if he lied, the Romans believed his hand would be bitten off; the Casa dei Crescenzi, residence of a medieval family; the Arco di Giano (Arch of Janus); and the ancient Tempio di Vesta (see **MONUMENTS 3, A-Z**) and Tempio della Fortuna Virile (see **MONUMENTS 3, A-Z**). See **SQUARES, WALK 3**.

Piazza del Campidoglio: This square and its *palazzi* lie in the dip between the twin summits of the Campidoglio (see **A-Z**) and were designed by Michelangelo (see **A-Z**). Steps from the Via del Teatro di Marcello lead up past statues of Castor and Pollux and the Emperor Constantine (see **A-Z**) and his son. At the back of the square is the Palazzo dei Senatori (official residence of the Mayor of Rome). On the left is the Palazzo Nuovo, and opposite is the Palazzo dei Conservatori. Together they house the Museo Capitolino (see **MUSEUMS 1, A-Z**). The bronze equestrian statue of Marcus Aurelius, which stood at the centre of the square, has been removed for restoration. See **SQUARES, WALK 4**.

Piazza Campo dei Fiori: One of the most ancient squares in Rome. It has a bloody history as a place of public execution. At its centre is a statue of the philosopher Giordano Bruno who was burnt at the stake for heresy in 1660. There are shops, a cinema and a daily fruit, vegetable and flower market. See **SHOPPING 1, SQUARES, WALK 4**.

Piazza Navona

Piazza Navona: One of the most popular squares in Rome, sited on the ancient Circus Agonalis (Domitian's athletic stadium). It is notable for the Fontana dei Fiumi (Fountain of the Four Rivers) by Bernini (see **A-Z**) and the church of S Agnese in Agone (see **CHURCHES 2**). In the Middle Ages it was popular for jousting, water pageants and horse races, and the carnival atmosphere persists as large crowds gather among the fountains to watch the various street artists and traders, or sit and chat in the cafés lining the square. See **SQUARES**, **WALK 4**.

Piazza del Popolo: Laid out in 1816-20 by Giuseppe Valadier. On the north side, beside the Porto del Popolo, is the church of S Maria del Popolo (see **CHURCHES 1**, **A-Z**); on the south side, flanking the *corso*, are the twin churches of S Maria di Monte Santo and S Maria dei Miracoli. In the centre is the Obelisco Flaminio, an Egyptian obelisk brought to Rome by the Emperor Augustus (see **A-Z**) for the Circo Massimo (see **A-Z**), and transferred here by Pope Sixtus V in 1589. See **SQUARES**.

Piazza San Pietro: The approach to St Peter's (see **CHURCHES 1**, **San Pietro in Vaticano**), enclosed by Bernini's (see **A-Z**) masterpiece, an oval colonnade four columns deep, surmounted by 140 statues of saints. In the centre is an obelisk erected by Domenico Fontana (1586), flanked by two fountains by Maderno (1613) and Fontana (1677).

Piazza di Spagna: The square takes its name from the Palazzo di Spagna, built in the 17thC to house the Spanish Ambassador to the Vatican (see **A-Z**). Today it is a popular meeting-point for visitors (and for crowds of young Romans too). It is best admired from the Via Condotti, or from the top of the Scalinata della Trinità dei Monti (Spanish Steps) in front of the church of Trinità dei Monti (see **A-Z**). The

Piazza di Spagna

Pincio

steps were built by Francesco de Santis between 1723-1726, and are usually crowded with tourists. The boat-shaped fountain was the work of Bernini's father (see **A-Z**), who supposedly conceived the idea when a boat was stranded here after the Tiber was flooded. See **SQUARES**.

Pincio: Public gardens laid out by Giuseppe Valadier in 1809-14 above the Piazza del Popolo (see **SQUARES**, **A-Z**) on land owned by the Pinci family (4thC). The view from the gardens over the *piazza* and the centre of the city are superb.

Piramide di Caio Cestio: The marble tomb of Tribune Caius Cestius, built in 12-11 BC, and later incorporated with the Porta San Paolo (see **A-Z**) into the Mura Aureliane (see **MONUMENTS 3**, **A-Z**). The pyramid is 22 m square and 27 m high, and was (according to the inscription) erected in 330 days. See **MONUMENTS 3**, **WALK 3**.

Police: There are several types of police in the city: the *Carabinieri* (tel: 212121), who deal with serious crimes; the *Policia* (tel: 67691), who deal with general crime and administrative problems, including lost passports and theft reports for insurance claims; and the *Vigili Urbani* and *Polizia Stradale*, who deal with traffic problems inside and outside the city respectively. See **Crime and Theft**, **Emergencies**.

Ponte Sant'Angelo: The most attractive of Rome's ancient bridges, built by Hadrian (see **A-Z**) in AD 134 (the three central arches survive from this period) to connect the Mausoleo di Adriano (Castel Sant'Angelo - see **MONUMENTS 1**, **MUSEUMS 1**, **A-Z**) with the old city. The ten statues of angels were added by Bernini (see **A-Z**) and his school in 1669-71. The bridge is a favourite spot with street traders. See **WALK 4**.

Porta Maggiore: City gate built in AD 52 by the Emperor Claudius at the point were the Via Prenestina and Via Labicana passed under two aqueducts: the Aqua Claudia and Anio Novus. It was later incorporated into the Mura Aureliane (see MONUMENTS 3, **A-Z**). Via Prenestina and Via Casilina.

Porta Pia: Built in 1561-5, it is one of the last masterpieces by Michelangelo (see **A-Z**). The exterior was restored in the 19thC. There is a military museum (Museo Storico dei Bersaglieri) housed in the outer sections. Via XX Settembre/Via Nomentana.

Porta San Pancrazio: Once the starting point for the Via Aurelia, it was erected in the 17thC by Pope Urban VIII and rebuilt in 1854 by Pius IX after it was badly damaged by fighting between Garibaldi and the French. Via Aurelia.

Porta San Paolo: Originally called the Porta Ostiense (3rdC AD), the gate is flanked by defensive towers built in the 6thC. Inside, the Museo della Via Ostiense illustrates the history of this important Roman thoroughfare. See WALK 3.

Porta San Sebastiano: Undoubtedly the best-preserved of the city gates (5thC AD). Flanked by its two imposing towers, it leads to the Via Appia Antica (see **A-Z**).

Post Offices: The Head Post Office, in Piazza San Silvestro, has a 24-hr telegram and international phone service (telex/fax) and *Poste Restante* facilities (0830-2100 Mon.-Fri., 0800-1200 Sat.). Stamps are sold at tobacconists (displaying a 'T' sign) and hotels as well as post offices. The current rate for a postcard to any EC country is L. 550 (L. 550 plus L. 300 for every 5 g to the USA), while a letter under 20 g costs L. 650 (L. 750 plus L. 300 for every 5 g to the USA). The Vatican City (see **A-Z**) has its own stamps and postmarks, and its own post office in the Piazza San Pietro (see **A-Z**). Postcards, *etc*, must be posted in the special blue post boxes in the Piazza or souvenir shops near the Vatican. See **Opening Times**, **Telephones and Telegrams**.

Public Holidays: Offices and shops are closed on Sundays and on the following public holidays: 1 Jan. (New Year); Easter Monday; 25 April (Liberation Day); 1 May (Labour Day); 15 Aug. (Assumption); 1 Nov. (All Saints' Day); 8 Dec. (Immaculate Conception); 25 Dec. (Christmas Day); 26 Dec. (St Stephen's Day).

Rabies: Still a danger here as in other areas of the Continent. As a precaution, have all animal bites examined by a doctor. See **Pets**.

Railways: Rome's main railway station is Stazione Termini, with direct services to Continental destinations and all the main Italian cities including Florence, Milan, Naples and Genova. Services are reliable and reasonably priced (enquire about discounts), tel: 4775 or contact the EPT office for information (see **Tourist Information**). The fastest trains are the *Trans Europe Express* (TEE) and the *Intercity* (IC), which stop at major destinations only (reserve in advance). The *Rapido* (R) and *Esprèsso* (ES) are also express services and only stop at large towns. The *Diretto* (D), *Locale* (L), *Accelerato* (A) and *Littorina* (L) are all fairly slow local services which stop frequently. Porters charge L. 700 per bag inside the station and L. 1650 from station to hotel.

Raphael (1483-1520): Born in Urbino, Raffaello Sanzio was a painter, sculptor and architect, but, like Michelangelo (see **A-Z**), he is best known for his paintings. In 1508 Julius II called him to Rome (where he remained for the rest of his life) to decorate the private papal apartments - *stanze* - in the Vatican (see **A-Z**). The first of these, the *Stanza della Segnatura* (see **MUSEUMS 2**), contains *The School of Athens,* one of his greatest works. In 1514 he succeeded Bramante as architect of St Peter's (see **CHURCHES 1**, **San Pietro in Vaticano**) but little of his architectural work survives unaltered.

Religious Services: *Roman Catholic Services* - Mass is celebrated up to 1300 and from 1700-2000 on Sundays (and often weekdays) in main churches; High Mass is celebrated in the seven basilicas on Sundays at 0930/1030; Roman Catholic Services in English are held in S Silvestro in Capite, St Thomas of Canterbury and S Susanna; confessions are

heard in English in the four main basilicas and in Il Gesù (see **CHURCHES 1**, **A-Z**), S Maria sopra Minerva (see **CHURCHES 2**) and S Sabina.
Anglican Church - All Saints, Via del Babuino 153/b.
American Episcopal - St Paul's, Via Nazionale.
Methodist Church - Ponte Sant'Angelo, Piazza Banco S Spirito 3.
Jewish Synagogue - Lungotevere dei Cenci.

Restaurants: There are literally thousands of eating-places in Rome ranging from elite establishments to simple trattorias serving cheap, local dishes. Pizzerias, *rosticcerie* (which serve hot snacks and take-aways), self-service and fast-food outlets are also widespread. A meal for two costs about L. 30,000-L. 60,000 (budget), L. 70,000-L. 100,000 (moderate), L. 120,000 and over (expensive). A service charge of around 15% is normally added to the bill. In some restaurants there is also a cover charge (*coperto*). See **RESTAURANTS**, **Food**.

San Clemente: Originally built over a 3rdC shrine of Mithras (itself housed in a 1stC domus) in the 4thC, it was later destroyed and a new basilica erected by Pope Pascal II (1099-1118). The triumphal arch and apse of the upper church are richly decorated with mosaics of biblical scenes. The lower church (4thC) contains a series of Romanesque (8th-12thC) wall paintings. On the lowest level are the partial excavations of the 1stC domus and Mithraic Temple. See **CHURCHES 2**.

San Giovanni in Laterano: This basilica is the cathedral church of Rome, and the seat of the Pope in his role as the Bishop of Rome. Very little remains of the original 4thC basilica, as this church has suffered more than any other in the city from the ravages of fires, sackings and earthquakes. Its present appearance dates from the 17th and 18thC. The Baroque facade was designed by Alessandro Galilei (c. 1735), and the interior by Borromini (see **A-Z**) in 1650. Its notable features include: the bronze doors, taken from the Curia in the Foro Romano (see **MONUMENTS 1**, **A-Z**); the superb timber ceiling; the 13thC mosiacs in the apse, by Jacopo Torriti; the bronze tomb of Martin V; and the magnificent Cosmatesque work (marble inlaid with coloured tiles) in the cloisters. See **CHURCHES 1**.

San Pietro in Montorio: Founded before the 9thC on the supposed site of St Peter's crucifixion (wrongly sited on the Gianicolo according to medieval legend), it was rebuilt after 1481 for King Ferdinand IV of Spain by Baccio Pontelli. The church is chiefly notable for the *Tempietto* (a circular columned building) added by Bramante (see **A-Z**) in 1502 in the small courtyard to the right of the church, a masterpiece of High Renaissance architecture. See **CHURCHES 2**.

San Pietro in Vaticano: The greatest church in Christendom and a magnet for pilgrims from all over the world. In 1505 Pope Julius II appointed Bramante (see **A-Z**) as architect of the new St Peter's to replace the original 4thC basilica erected by Constantine near the site of the Apostle's martyrdom (c. 64). Bramante's Greek cruciform design remained incomplete at his death in 1516, and the work was taken over by Raphael (see **A-Z**), Peruzzi and Antonio da Sangallo the Younger until the intervention of Michelangelo (see **A-Z**) whose simple design of a square cross with dome superseded competing plans. Only the drum of the dome was completed before he died, and the finished

San Pietro in Vaticano

design owes much to Giacomo della Porta. In 1605 Paul V commissioned Carlo Maderno to add a nave and facade, and the church was finally completed in 1626 and consecrated by Urban VIII. From the central balcony on the facade the Pope delivers his *Urbi et Orbi* blessing (see **Events**). The portico contains five entrances to the church, the Porta Santa being opened only in a Holy Year. Inside, the first chapel to the right contains Michelangelo's famous *Pietà* (1499) protected by glass since being attacked by an assailant with a hammer in 1972. The Baroque interior is largely the work of Bernini (see **A-Z**), whose magnificent bronze *baldacchino* (canopy) towers above the high altar. In the apse is Bernini's bronze *Throne of St Peter* flanked by Patristic figures, and below are the tombs of Paul III to the left (G. della Porta, 1551-75), and of Urban VIII to the right (Bernini, 1642-7). Notable treasures in the left aisle include: the *Tomb of Alexander VII* (Bernini, 1672-78); the *Cappella della Colonna* (1646-50); the *Tomb of Leo XI Medici* (A. Algardi, 1642-44); and the *Stuart Monument* (Canova 1817-19). There is a lift to the roof of the church, which commands a spectacular view. From the roof, steps lead to the lantern, allowing a close view of Michelangelo's dome. You can also descend to the Sacre Grotte Vaticane (Vatican Grottoes), containing the tombs of many popes. See **CHURCHES 1**.

San Pietro in Vincoli: Started in 431, this is one of the city's oldest churches, although it was considerably altered in later centuries. In a reliquary under the high altar are preserved the chains which supposedly bound St Peter during his imprisonment in Jerusalem. The greatest works of art in the church are the statues carved by Michelangelo (see **A-Z**) for the tomb of Julius II, the magnificent figure of *Moses* flanked by *Leah* and *Rachel*. See **CHURCHES 3**, **WALK 2**.

Santa Costanza: Near Sant'Agnese fuori le Mura (see **CHURCHES 1**), this church was originally built in the 4thC as a mausoleum for Helena and Constantia, daughters of Constantine (see **A-Z**), but was consecrated in 1254. The central dome is carried by twelve double columns and the tunnel-vaulted ambulatory is decorated with exquisite mosaics combining Christian and pagan subjects. Via Nomentana. Bus 36 from Stazione Termini (see **Railways**).

Santa Maria in Aracoeli: The Franciscans built this church in 1250 on the site of an 8thC monastery on the highest summit of the Campidoglio (see **A-Z**), a sacred spot since history began. Its name is taken from the altar - *ara coeli* - which, according to legend, was raised by Augustus (see **A-Z**) after he experienced a vision of the Madonna and Child here. The steep flight of 122 steps leading to the church from the Piazza d'Aracoeli dates from 1348. The painting on the ceiling is the *Victory at Lepanto* (1571) by Marcantonio Colonna, and also notable are frescoes by Pinturicchio depicting the *Life of St Bernardino* and the *Santo Bambino* in the Chapel of the Holy Child. See CHURCHES 2.

Santa Maria in Cosmedin: One of Rome's most attractive medieval churches, situated in the Piazza Bocca della Verità (see SQUARES, **A-Z**). Dating from the 6thC and enlarged in the 8thC, its present form is due to 12thC modifications. The seven-storey campanile, Cosmatesque pavement, choir and portico date from this period. The portico contains the Bocca della Verità (Mouth of Truth), used as a trial by ordeal in the Middle Ages, which is supposed to bite off the fingers of liars whose hands are placed in its mouth. See CHURCHES 2, WALK 3.

Santa Maria Maggiore: One of the four patriarchal basilicas, it sits on the summit of the Esquilino, and was built by Sixtus III (432-40) in honour of the Virgin Mary, after the Council of Ephasis (431) promoted veneration of the Virgin. The nave is lined with 40 classical columns and the superb coffered ceiling is supposedly gilded with the first gold brought from the exploration of America. It has a superb Cosmatesque pavement, and 5thC mosaics above the architrave and altar and lavishly ornamented Baroque Sistine and Pauline chapels. The campanile dates from 1377 and, at 75 m, is the highest in Rome. See CHURCHES 1, WALK 2.

Santa Maria del Popolo: This church contains some of the city's greatest works of art, many of them commissioned by Pope Sixtus IV and other members of the della Rovere family. The original 11thC foundation was rebuilt by Sixtus IV in 1474, and the interior was later remodelled by Bernini (see **A-Z**). The most notable paintings are those by Pinturicchio in the della Rovere chapel and two works by Caravaggio (see **A-Z**), the *Conversion of St Paul* and the *Crucifixion of St Peter,* in the first chapel of the left transept. There are also works by Annibale Caracci, Raphael (see **A-Z**), Sansovino, Bernini and Sebastiano del Piombo. See **CHURCHES 1**.

Shopping: The best (and most expensive) shops are situated in the streets around the Piazza di Spagna (see **SQUARES**, **A-Z**). These include top outlets for fashion wear, shoes, jewellery, furs and leather garments and accessories. The Via Coronari is famous for its antique shops selling furniture, silver, jewellery, pictures, *etc,* and a similar selection can be found along the Via del Babuino. There is also a small shopping area near the Pantheon (see **MONUMENTS 1**, **WALK 4**, **A-Z**) which is less expensive. Most shops will happily arrange to post purchases abroad. See **SHOPPING**, **Best Buys**, **Opening Times**.

Sistine Chapel: See **Cappella Sistina**.

Spanish Steps: See **Piazza di Spagna**.

Sports: The Foro Italico sports complex (1931), north of Monte Mario, contains the Stadio Olimpico where football teams from Rome and Lazio play every other Sunday afternoon, Sept.-May. The stadium can hold crowds of up to 100,000. There are also open-air and enclosed swimming pools, lawn tennis and basketball courts, running tracks and many other facilities. Another sports centre, the Tre Fontane at EUR (see **A-Z**) contains the Piscina delle Rose, a 50 m open-air swimming pool (Viale America; 0900-1230, 1400-1900 daily June-Sept. M EUR Marconi. L. 5000-L. 8000). There is horse racing at Tor di Valle (9 km south west on Via del Mare), and an international horse show is held in the Villa Borghese (see **A-Z**) in April-May.

Taxis: Taxis are yellow and must be hired from ranks or summoned by telephone: *Radio Taxi Romana,* tel: 3570; *Radio Taxi La Capitale,* tel: 4994. There are supplements for extra luggage, for night service (2200-0700), and on Sundays and holidays. A small tip is expected.

Teatro di Marcello: Begun by Julius Caesar (see **A-Z**) and completed by Augustus (see **A-Z**) in 13 BC for his nephew and son-in-law Marcellus. Due to its robust construction and strategic position overlooking the Tiber it was converted into a fortress in the 12thC, partially incorporated into a *palazzo* in the 16thC, and eventually passed into the possession of the Orsini family in 1712. Although only 12 of its original 41 arches in two tiers survive, it remains one of the city's most impressive monuments. See MONUMENTS 2, WALK 3.

Telephones and Telegrams: You will find public telephones on many streets, in railway stations, in bars and newsagents (displaying the yellow sign), at the Centro Telefonico Pubblico (SIP) in Stazione Termini (see **Railways**) and Piazza San Silvestro (near the main post office). Newer coin-operated phones take L. 100, 200 and 500 coins. Other phones use phone cards worth L. 1000 and L. 5000, which can be purchased at tobacconists, but some of the older ones still only accept tokens (*gettoni*), which can be purchased in bars, hotels, newsagents, tobacconists and post offices for L. 200. It is best to make international calls from the main post offices or SIP kiosks. To direct dial abroad, first dial 00 followed by the code for the country (UK - 44, USA - 1), then remember to omit the first 0 of the city code before dialling the rest of the number. There is a 24-hr telegram service at the head post office (see **Post Offices**), or you can send one by phone (tel: 186). A cheaper, more efficient alternative is a night letter/telegram which is guaranteed to arrive the following morning.

Tempio della Fortuna Virile: Elegant and well-preserved 2ndC BC temple close to the Tempio di Vesta (see **A-Z**) on the east bank of the Tiber. Piazza Bocca della Verità. See MONUMENTS 3, WALK 3.

Tempio di Vesta: A circular temple close to the Tempio della Fortuna Virilis (see MONUMENTS 3, **A-Z**). Its name derives from the resemblance it bears to the Temple of Vesta in the Foro Romano (see MONUMENTS 1, WALK 1, **A-Z**). Dating from the 2ndC BC, it is the oldest surviving marble temple in Rome. Piazza Bocca della Verità. See MONUMENTS 3, WALK 1, WALK 3.

Terme di Caracalla: Ancient Rome's equivalent of today's public baths were in fact much more than just baths. There were exercise rooms, a stadium, three large pools (with cold, tepid and hot water), two libraries, an art gallery, and a pleasure garden. The baths (completed by the Emperor Caracalla in AD 216) could accommodate up to 1600 bathers. Little remains of the original, lavishly decorated interior, as it was comprehensively looted by the Farnese family - note the two huge vascas, converted into fountains, which now sit in front of the Palazzo Farnese (see WALK 4, **A-Z**). See MONUMENTS 2.

Terme di Diocleziano: Similar to the Terme di Caracalla (see **A-Z**), but even larger, built to serve the northern district of the city and completed by the Emperor Diocletian in 305-306. The remains are now incorporated into a variety of buildings, including the church of S Maria degli Angeli, designed by Michelangelo (see **A-Z**), and part of the baths now houses the Museo Nazionale Romano (see MUSEUMS 1, **A-Z**). See MONUMENTS 2.

Time Differences: GMT + 1 hr in winter, GMT + 2 hrs in summer.

Tipping: Although restaurant, café and hotel bills usually include a service charge, it is customary to leave a 10% tip if you are happy with the service. Taxi drivers, cinema and theatre ushers, hairdressers, toilet attendants and guides also expect to be tipped. Porters should be given L. 1000 per item of luggage.

Tivoli: A delightful town 32 km north east of Rome set on the lower slopes of the Sabine hills overlooking the Campagna Romana. Known as *Tibur* in classical times, many patrician Roman families chose this area for their summer villas. Its main attraction today is the 16thC Villa d'Este, with its terraced garden and cascading fountains. Also worth visiting is the Villa Gregoriana, built for Pope Gregory XVI in the 19thC, and the Grande Cascata, a 120 m-high, artificial waterfall. Nearby are the ruins of the Tempio di Vesta, dating from the Republican period, and the earlier Tempio della Sibilla. 6 km south of the town is the Villa Adriana (see **Hadrian**), and a visit to the Villa and Tivoli is an ideal day-

Villa d'Este, Tivoli

out from Rome. There is a regular bus service to Tivoli from Piazza dei Cinquecento, outside Stazione Termini (see **Railways**), and to the Villa Adriana from Piazza della Repubblica. Buses also run regularly between the Villa and Tivoli. See **EXCURSION 3**.

Tourist Information: The Ente Nazionale il Turismo (ENIT) office Via Marghera 2, tel: 4971222/82 will help you with any queries and advise you on such matters as accommodation. They also provide free maps. The regional office, Ente Provinciale per il Turismo (EPT), for Rome is at Via Parigi 11, tel: 461851 (0820-1340 Mon.-Fri., 0820-1330 Sat.), and there are branches at Stazione Termini (see **Railways**), Fiumicino Airport arrivals hall (see **Airports**), and at motorway service areas at Saleria Ovest (on the A 1 from Milan/Florence) and Frascati Est (on the A 2 from Naples).

Tours: Various travel agencies run tours of the city and to the Castelli Romani (see **EXCURSION 1**), Cerveteri, Tivoli (see **EXCURSION 3**, **A-Z**), Bracciano (see **EXCURSION 4**, **A-Z**) and other places. *Carrani Tours,* Via V. E. Orlando 95 (tel: 4742501) run coach tours in the city and environs with multilingual guides; *Walk History* (tel: 4750731/ 0774-8387666) arrange guided walking tours of the city; *Tourvisa* (tel: 493481) run summer boat trips along the Tiber (April-Sept.) and to Ostia Antica (see EXCURSION 2, **A-Z**); *ATAC* (see **Buses**) run bus tours of the city from the terminus outside the station (bus 110, L. 6000). Guided tours of the Vatican (see **A-Z**) are also available. Contact the EPT (see **Tourist Information**) for more details.

Transport: The best way of getting around the city, apart from walking (since there is so much to see within a relatively small area), is by local bus or tram. The *Metropolitana* (Underground) has only two lines and is of limited use for tourists. In summer you can hire a horse-drawn carriage (*carrozzella*) in Piazza di Spagna (see SQUARES, **A-Z**) or outside the Colosseo (see MONUMENTS 1, WALK 1, **A-Z**) - establish the fare before you set off. To explore the towns and countryside around Rome you will need to hire a car or book a coach excursion. There are also reliable bus and train services to destinations throughout the region. The best means of intercity travel is the train, which is fast, reliable and good value. See **Buses**, **Car Hire**, **Driving**, **Railways**, **Taxis**, **Tours**.

Trastevere: A lively and increasingly fashionable district 'across the Tiber' of narrow streets and small houses and squares. It was traditionally the home of artisans and dock workers, and the inhabitants claim to possess a more ancient and purer Roman ancestry than residents on the other side of the Tiber. In July the festival of *Noiantri* 'we others' is held to celebrate this difference. See CITY DISTRICTS, WALK 3.

Traveller's Cheques: See **Money**.

Trevi Fountain: See **Fontana di Trevi**.

Trinità dei Monti: Dominating the Piazza di Spagna (see SQUARES, **A-Z**) and the Spanish Steps, this church was founded by Louis XII of France in 1502 and completed in 1587. The Baroque facade is by Carlo Maderno, and inside in the Cappella Orsini is the fresco of *The Deposition* (c. 1541) by Daniele da Volterra, regarded as his masterpiece. Piazza Trinità dei Monti. M Spagna.

Vatican City (Città del Vaticano): Population: c. 1000. An independent sovereign state established by the Lateran Treaty of 1929 between the Holy See and Mussolini. Surrounded by walls except for St Peter's (see **CHURCHES 1, San Pietro in Vaticano**) and the Piazza San Pietro (see **A-Z**), it covers 43 hectares. Legislative, executive and judicial authority resides with the Pope, who has his own bodyguard (Swiss Guard) who wear brightly-coloured medieval uniforms. The Vatican has its own post office, bank, newspaper, radio station, railway station and shops. Apart from the museums (see **MUSEUMS 2, A-Z**) St Peter's, and other specific areas, entrance is forbidden without permission.

Musei Vaticani

Vatican Museums (Musei Vaticani): One of the world's greatest art collections, housed largely in the Vatican Palace. The collection was started by Pope Julius II in 1503 and contains works acquired by or gifted to the Papacy down to the present day. See **MUSEUMS 2**.

Via Appia Antica: The principal Roman consular road, built in 312 BC by Appius Claudius to link Rome with south-east Italy and, through the port of Brindisi, to Greece. The tombs of rich Roman families are dotted along the road, as burials were not permitted within the city walls. Most of the tombs have been plundered by grave-robbers, or incorporated into later churches and other buildings. Apart from the Catacombs (see **A-Z**), worth seeing are the little church of Domine Quo

Vadis (supposedly on the site where St Peter was met by a vision of Jesus and returned to the city and martyrdom) and the Tomb of Cecilia Metella (1stC BC). Bus 118 from the Colosseo (see **MONUMENTS 1**, **A-Z**).

Villa Borghese: A large and splendid area of parkland created in the 17thC by Cardinal Scipione Borghese. There are woodlands, fountains, lakes, landscaped gardens, a small zoo (see **Children**) and the Pincio (see **A-Z**).

Villa Farnesina: An elegant Renaissance villa built in 1510 by Peruzzi, for the Sienese banker Chigi. See the superb frescoed ceilings by Raphael (see **A-Z**), and the famous etchings by Piranesi in the Gabinetto delle Stampe. Via della Lungara 230. 0900-1300 Mon.-Sat. Bus 23, 65 from Piazza Venezia (see **SQUARES**, **WALK 1**, **A-Z**).

Villa Giulia: Built as a pleasant retreat for Pope Julius III in 1553, this building now houses the Museo Nazionale di Villa Giulia, the most important collection of Etruscan art in the world (see **MUSEUMS 1**). The many works of art displayed include a superb terracotta statue of Apollo and Hercules, and a beautiful sarcophagus with the smiling figures of a husband and wife reclining together. The villa itself is a Renaissance masterpiece, with a facade by Vignola, and many charming features by Bartolomeo Ammannati and Giorgio Vasari.

What's On: For information on events in Rome check the listings in the following publications: *La Settimana a Roma* (available in English as *This Week in Rome*), Friday's *Il Messaggero* and *Trovaroma* in Saturday's *La Repubblica*. Listings are also published in *Wanted in Rome*, a free English-language newsletter which appears every two weeks and is distributed to bars, restaurants and newsagents.

Youth Hostels: The only hostel in Rome is the *Ostello del Foro Italico*, Viale delle Olimpiadi 61 (350 beds) tel: 3964909. There is also the *Y.W.C.A.*, Via C. Balbo 4; and the *Salvation Army*, Via degli Apuli 39/41. For more details of cheap accommodation, contact EPT offices (see **Tourist Information**).

The publishers welcome corrections and suggestions from readers; write to:
The Publishing Manager, Travel Guides, Collins Publishers, PO Box, Glasgow G4 ONB